PERSONAL
EXCELLENCE
THROUGH THE
BHAGAVAD GITA

Nalini

PERSONAL EXCELLENCE
THROUGH THE
BHAGAVAD GITA

SWAMI
SUKHABODHANANDA

JAICO PUBLISHING HOUSE

Ahmedabad Bangalore Bhopal Bhubaneswar Chennai
Delhi Hyderabad Kolkata Lucknow Mumbai

Published by Jaico Publishing House
A-2 Jash Chambers, 7-A Sir Phirozshah Mehta Road
Fort, Mumbai - 400 001
jaicopub@jaicobooks.com
www.jaicobooks.com

Published in arrangement with
Prasanna Trust
No. 51, 16th Cross, Between 6th & 8th Main
Malleswaram, Bangalore 560 003, India

PERSONAL EXCELLENCE THROUGH THE BHAGAVAD GITA
ISBN 978-81-7992-731-1

First Jaico Impression: 2007
Ninth Jaico Impression: 2011

Printed by
Snehesh Printers
320-A, Shah & Nahar Ind. Est. A-1
Lower Parel, Mumbai - 400 013.

ABOUT THE AUTHOR

- **Swami Sukhabodhananda** is the founder Chairman of Prasanna Trust. He is also the founder of the research wing of Prasanna Foundation, which focuses on the scientific aspects of meditation.

- His several books have made many discover a new way of living life. He makes you realise that if one door closes another door opens. Life is an opening.

- He is a regular invitee to various forums in India, USA, UK, and Switzerland.

- He has been addressing many gatherings at important Universities in India and abroad.

- Leading industrial houses invite him to conduct 'In-house workshops' for their executives.

- His self-development programs have benefited many in the corporate sectors of reputed institutions like banking, finance, industry, education, armed forces and police.

- "Times of India" in their recent poll on "who talks the best" places Swamiji as the one, who tops the list on all counts as the best speaker.

- "The Week" magazine acclaims Swamiji as one among the top five best exponent of spiritual knowledge.

- Swamiji's English books "Oh, Mind Relax Please!" and "Oh, Life Relax Please!" are the top best-sellers in the country and has set a new bench mark in the lives of many, from the Kargil hero Gen. V. P. Malik who swear by the inspiring content of the book to the New York Mayor who acknowledges its usefulness to diminish work pressure and dealing with New York City press!

- His other English books are marching best-sellers.

- Swamiji's book "Manase Relax Please" has set an all time sales record in the history of Tamil, Kannada & Telugu books and has been included as a part of curriculum in some of the schools & colleges. Leading personalities have termed that he has revolutionized Tamil literature through his books.

- Swamiji was invited as a dignitary on five different panels at the World Economic Forum in Davos, Switzerland and was a special invitee to the United Nation World Millennium Summit of spiritual Leaders.

- Swamiji is the only Hindu monk who was invited to participate in the program "Eye on India" showcasing the country by CNN.

- Swamiji's works in audio and video have been transforming the lives of many through Sa Re Ga Ma and Times Music.

- His message on the Astha, Gemini, Sadhana, DD Chandana, World Space Radio and many other Channels is reaching a wide spectrum of people both in India and Overseas.

- Swamiji was awarded 'Karnataka's Best Social Service Award' by Essel group & Zee network.

FROM THE AUTHOR

I have always inspired myself that if I cannot be happy 'here and now,' I will never be happy anywhere. This book is an offering of my insights to create happiness in all walks of life. This is possible if one looks at life in a new way.... looking at life differently.

The superficial way of reading this book is through intellectual understanding. The deeper way is by feeling the insights of the narration. The deepest way is where these insights and parables light up your mind and heart in your hours of darkness and guide you like a spiritual friend.

Hence I invite you to read this book not just once, but many times over like a daily prayer... for prayer does not change the Lord but changes you.

By ingesting the essence of this book, you will realise what lies before you and behind you are nothing in comparison to what lies within you. Enlightenment is looking for spectacles that sit right on your nose. Enlightenment is always 'here and now,' never in the past or future. This book attempts to awaken you... like a wake up call.

To do what you like and like what you do is indeed a divine work. Work is an opportunity to find oneself. This book helps you in finding your 'self' in all walks *of life... family, work, social, and spiritual zones. In the process, you will be grateful to the weeds of your mind. They ultimately help your practice of relaxation.*

Being relaxed is wise. Begin with being wise and you will be relaxed. Being relaxed is a wise and an easy way to live life. When you are relaxed, you look at life differently.

Life, thus lived will bring forth the peace of a rose garden and light of the luminous Sun as a part of your being.

Let your growth bring the best seasons of your life. This is my humble prayer for you.

I specially thank P. R. Madhav for editing this book. My special thanks to Mrs. Devki Jaipuria for all her support. My salutation to my loving mother who is the source of my inspiration. My deepest gratitude, which cannot be expressed in words, goes out to all my Gurus. I offer this book to all my students who are like little lamps shining in the night, which the great Sun cannot do. This is my dream and I am sure you will join me in making it as your destination.

With blessings,

SWAMI SUKHABODHANANDA

CONTENTS

ix

Contents

1

AWARENESS
THE INNER ALCHEMY

ow, in adding life to our years what is it that is really involved? It involves a certain level of deep awareness. If that certain level of deep awareness is not there, then, please understand, you may assume that you are growing up, where in fact you are only growing old and therefore the whole punch line of philosophy in one word is nothing but awareness. And at the second level, how do you take this awareness and apply it in your daily life?

Just like how a musician increases his awareness and converts sounds into a melody. By sheer awareness he converts sounds into a melody; so too, a person awakened inside takes experiences with awareness, puts them into a harmony and creates melody.

Hence the Veda says "Rasovai saha," your whole being can be "Rasovai saha," extremely juicy if you know how to do it. You do not change your experiences – we are usually busy in changing the experiences, but what the Gita says is change your inner state of being rather than changing events in life. When you change your inner state of being, then you find that, like a musician, you will be able to put those experiences into a certain harmony which will create melody in life and that is what is called "Rasovai Saha."

The Veda says your whole being is going to become "juicy," so the whole game is about awareness. But this word, awareness, can also be a very, very mechanical term, a conceptual term, and not an experiential term, like how God has been a conceptual term for a lot of people and not an experiential one. God can be a concept or an experience, Love can be a concept or an experience, Bliss can be either a concept or an experience and in knowing the distinction between a concept and an experience and in keeping the vision to transform a concept into an experience lies the acuity of living life dexterously... in the Gita way.

There was once a very religious person who was spreading the message of God everywhere and therefore his Guru, his Master who taught him the A, B, C of God and religion, came to him and said, "You have spread the message of God so beautifully, as a token on your birthday I am going to give you a black Arabian horse as a gift," because this religious person was a lover of horses. So the Guru gives a beautiful Arabian horse as a gift and then tells his student, "There is only one condition –this horse is a very religious horse because it has been living with me and therefore it knows only two words – 'Oh God' and 'Hallelujah.' If you want the horse to gallop you have to say 'Oh God,' and it will start galloping and whipping the horse is not going to help, and if you want the horse to stop then pulling the reins is not going to help – you have to say 'Hallelujah,' and the moment you say 'Hallelujah,' abruptly it will stop. So to run you have to say 'Oh God' and to stop you have to say 'Hallelujah.' "

Both are very religious terms. And therefore this man says, "I have learnt so many scriptures, so what is so difficult about these two terms;" so he sits on the black Arabian horse because he is a lover of horses, and says, "Oh God," and the horse starts galloping, galloping, and galloping.

He says, "Oh God, Oh God, Oh God," and at lightning speed the horse gallops, and gallops and gallops. He gets into a state of euphoria. He can't even imagine that this is happening because the horse is going at lightning speed.

Then he remembers and becomes aware that the horse that is going at such lightning speed has not got the intelligence to slow down when it is at the edge of a cliff, and because it is almost at the edge of a cliff he presses his panic button and pulls the reins. But to his surprise, it does not stop and yet it is going to the edge of the cliff at lightning speed and it is not stopping.

Then, fortunately, his memory works. To stop you have to say "Hallelujah," and he says "Hallelujah," and abruptly it stops right at the edge of the cliff. He looks down and sees thousands of feet below the cliff – one mistake means in one second he would have gone down that lane. He looks up and says, "Oh God, thank you," and the horse gallops.

Even the words "Oh God" are so mechanical.

2

DON'T CREATE A CONFLICT WITHIN CONFLICT

am trying to convey through this a distinction that is important for personal excellence and this is something Lord Krishna goes on saying, so you should note the distinction very clearly. A menu card is not the biryani. A menu card is not the idli. On the menu the dish "idli" is written. You can't eat that idli; you have to order it to eat it. So a word is only a concept and the verses of the Gita are not only concepts – they are great words but unless you convert them into your experience, it is not going to help.

The greatest catastrophe that has happened to religion is this – it has become words, it has become concepts, it has become dogmas and opinions, it has become belief systems but it has still not become an experience, and the greatest harm we are doing to religion is that we are converting it into a belief system. We have tremendous respect for the Gita, but are we living the Gita? To live, it is the most important thing to bring about personal excellence.

You talk of love but every action is other than love. Love is that which unifies, but then we start talking of division. I am this caste; which caste are you? I am this religion or that

5

one, and therefore the whole catastrophe has happened. Right at the outset I want you to be aware that the word Gita, and the word God, should not just become a concept. It should not be a conceptual understanding; it should be an existential understanding.

Why is it that we listen to so much, yet the listening does not bring about a transformation in us? We listen to so many discourses of the Gita, read the Bhagavad Gita, then why does it not become a process of an inner alchemy? It is all because we have not created a spiritual apparatus. Please understand that for this alchemy to happen just listening is not going to be enough. "Atmavare shrotavyam" – first learn to listen; then you have to go into "mantavyam," you have to learn to reflect; then "nidhidyasitavyam," you should learn to meditate. So you are listening, then reflecting, then meditating on it and living it, and for this a spiritual apparatus has to be created.

In one of our ancient texts we have a beautiful story which I will relate to you as an example. Please reflect on this.

There was a king, a much respected king and he had a guru who was a monk, a fakir. He used to come every day, and give him a forest fruit, a wild forest fruit. Now when you look at the forest fruit it looks very gross. It is not like an apple or an orange. So when the guru gave it he took it and then, when the guru went away he just threw it in the basement.

Every day the guru used to come and give him a wild forest fruit, and he would put it in the basement. And this happened for a month, two months, and three months. And one day this king said to himself, "Hey, I just keep putting it in the basement and now I have to throw them all from the basement itself." So when the fakir gave him, once again, a fruit, and went away, he gave the fruit to his monkey. He had a palace monkey. The monkey started eating the fruit, and when it opened it, there inside was a huge diamond.

And then an understanding happened, an enlightenment happened and the king thought, "My God, all along my guru has been giving me fruit, I have been thinking it is a wild fruit, a gross fruit and putting it in the basement, but in the fruit there is a diamond – I have been only seeing the outer layer, I have not being seeing the inner layer. What a mistake I have made." He rushed to the basement. There he opened fruit after fruit and every fruit had a diamond, and then he realised how he had been discarding the wonderful gifts the guru had been giving.

With tears in his eyes he took his horse, galloped to the guru, bowed down to him, and apologised to him and the guru blessed him and said, "Friend, this is what is exactly happening to humanity."

Every moment God is blessing us with an experience, every moment there is an experience but we see only the periphery, we see the outer layer, and treat it as if it is a wild fruit but we miss the message which is hidden in the experience. Every moment in your marriage, in your divorce, in giving birth to your child, or a child even passing away, in every experience, if you see the outer only it seems to be like a wild fruit but if you go deep inside there is a divine message which is given. This is the message I want to convey to you through this story.

Now, this story goes on and there are deeper meanings

that come out in it. The king was none other than Veera Vikramaditya, and the guru says, "Come and meet me in a graveyard at midnight." There, he sees his guru – a tantrik mystic with dead bodies all around. He tells Vikramaditya, "Go a little deeper into the graveyard forest and you will find a tree with a corpse, a *vetal*, hanging from it. Then I want you to cut it, for which you should be very alert, and silent – in *mouna*. Then, keep the *vetal* on your shoulder and meet me here."

So, the king goes there, takes the sword and cuts the connection between the corpse and the tree, and when he puts *vetal* on his shoulder, it starts laughing, and laughing and laughing.

Then Veera Vikramaditya, unable to control his silence, asked, "Why are you laughing?" Immediately the *vetal* gets re-connected to the tree. Because – what was the condition? You should be aware and you should be in silence (*mouna*). The story goes on that Vikramaditya again cuts it, puts it on the shoulder and starts walking and it starts telling riddles in the form of beautiful stories, saying, "If you know the answer and don't tell me, I will kill you." And if he answers the *vetal* it goes back to the tree. It continues until a riddle was not answered by the king, and then the story goes on further. But for our present purpose, we look at two things from the story – be very aware and also be silent.

The 11th verse of the 2nd chapter of the Gita starts with "ashochyanan" (you grieve over those who should not be grieved about) and ends with "nanushochanti" (do not grieve). The whole message of the Gita is remove your "shoka," your sorrow, and the message is that the sorrow is eliminated if you remove the cause of the sorrow. What is the cause of the sorrow? "Shokasya karanam mohaha," the cause of your sorrow, is delusion (*moha*), and therefore the essence of the Gita is eliminate your sorrow (*shoka*) by removing the cause which is delusion (*moha*). When delusion (*moha*) is eliminated sorrow (*shoka*) is eliminated. There is nothing more purifying than understanding, says the Lord and therefore, for personal excellence, if this understanding, this knowledge has to dawn, you have two conditions to meet – one, you have to be extremely aware like Veera Vikramaditya and secondly, inwardly very silent. Then you will experience the purifying effect of understanding: "Nahi gnanena sadrusham pavithram iha vidyathe," as the sloka says.

If you are not aware and not silent you are not going to gain wisdom, you will only gain concepts. Lots of people think if they can rattle off the Gita, quote the mantra, they are wise, but the rattling off of the Gita and quoting of the mantra without being existentially aware and without being inwardly silent, is going to be only words, words and words.

The word is not the thing; the description is not the described, says the great thinker J. Krishnamurthy. Please get this very clearly before I start dwelling on personal excellence. For lots of people who have read the Gita it has just become words, so if it has to be more than words, be alert, be inwardly silent. When you are alert and silent inside, if you understand, well and good; if you don't understand, don't worry. For Hindus it is no problem. This "*janma*," this birth, is not the only one, we have many births, whereas other people have only one birth to exhaust. That is why Hindus are very relaxed people; many births, several *janmas*, are there for them.

9

Therefore don't worry; but just being relaxed is only one part; you have also to be aware. If you do not understand right now certain points I am making, be relaxed about it, don't get worried because worry is like a rocking chair – it keeps you busy but leads you nowhere. So don't worry. This is the first control, (*nigraha*), you should have. But if you don't worry when the whole house is burning, that is the irresponsible type of silence – please see these distinctions, because the graveyard silence is there and the silence of a rose garden is also there.

So, if you don't understand, firstly, don't worry, but that is not enough – secondly, become more aware. Just like the story of Vikramaditya. Be more aware, at the same time be silent and if you are aware and if you are silent, these two join and mix together and a certain synergy is created. When such synergy gets created, you don't get just knowledge (*gnanam*), you get wisdom (*vignanam*). For personal excellence just knowledge is not enough. You need "*gnana*" and also "*vignana*," which means intelligence. Your knowledge should result in intelligence. Knowledge repeats like a parrot but intelligence is a different ball game altogether.

And when you have intelligence, the Lord is going to say, even in a conflicting situation you can be in harmony and this is the principle of warfare. The meditative type of warfare is, in a conflict, don't create a conflict.

For example, you get angry; when you get angry then you get angry that you are angry; then double-decker anger; then you feel guilty that you are angry, so you are angry. Then you get upset that you feel guilty, so you are angry.

Then you get ashamed that you have attended so many

workshops of Swamiji and paid thousands of rupees, all wasted, and then you are again upset. Then, "*dabba pe dabba pe dabba*," layer on layer, and you feel miserable. Instead of that, when you get angry, create a harmony with that anger.

When you create a harmony with anger you experience anger, and the moment you experience anger you see its causes. When you see the cause of anger the very cause will be defused. When you remove the cause, the effect is gone. "Karana abhave karya abavahah." Therefore, in martial art there is a simple thing which is also part of the essence of the Gita – don't create a conflict in a conflict, create a harmony in a conflict.

3

HARMONY IN CONFLICT – CREATE A HARMONY IN CONFLICT

ord Krishna says, "Yaha sarvatra anabhis snehaha" – don't get attached to success or failure. When you are not attached to success or failure you are in a state of peace with whatever is to be, "shuba ashubam," be it the good or bad, which means conflict. Even in a conflict create a harmony.

I avoid using too much of Sanskrit so that you don't get a new tension called Sanskrit tension, but trust me, what I am saying is the Bhagavad Gita, and in between I will give slices of it or else you will think it is only my version that I am talking.

I will just introduce the verse, and afterwards you can refer the books properly. If I do an enquiry into the verse it will take a lot of time, and I am covering here just the top layer of personal excellence.

So the verse is:

Yaha sarvatra anabhisnehaha tattatprapya shubhashubham
Nabhi nandati na dvesti tasya prajna pratisthita.

Here, "Yaha sarvatra anabhis snehaha," only means

create a harmony in conflict. I am a student of martial art and in my workshop I demonstrate what happens when somebody tries to attack you.

The first lesson I learnt from my master was if somebody holds your neck or attacks you, first try to relax, because the maximum that will happen is you will die, and anyway you are going to die, so by relaxing you will die better. When he holds you and pushes you here and there, first be relaxed. Once you are relaxed, you are centered. Please get this word, which is used in martial art. You are centered. Once you are centered, as you are relaxing, the next step is to enter and break the other's center; you enter and break other's center of gravity.

That is why policemen don't hit drunkards, because they are so relaxed that if you hit them they will just fall. But when you become very conscious and fall you become rigid and when you become rigid you get injured. So this is the first thing in martial art and warfare. Once you don't resist you are going with the flow.

When you are going with the flow you are centered and once you are centered, then you poke the other's eyes, hit his throat and smash his jaws in that flow. Therefore the whole principle is this ... for personal excellence, create a harmony in conflict.

With a relaxed atmosphere, look at the mind. Your personal excellence will not grow when you are in tension. A lot of people who do my workshop, when they sit down for meditation and I say, "Close your eyes," invariably they open one eye because closing the eyes is so difficult for them, because their mind is going on chattering, you know, so they don't close their eyes. They close one eye, and I say, "Please close both your eyes." I initially get confused whether they understand my accent or not, so I say, "Eyes are two holes above your nose. Please close your eyes." Then they close their eyes.

Invariably quite a few people say, "Swamiji, when I close my eyes I am so much in tension." What is happening? "Thoughts which I never thought are coming now. I am tensed because I paid to attend your workshop and all is wasted now because I am thinking of rubbish." It is conflict for him because he is thinking of rubbish and the amount paid is wasted as I am teaching meditation. Such a conflicting situation ... and he has respect for me because Swamiji is going to teach meditation and he is becoming mad with reference to meditation. So it is a conflicting situation. I tell them a beautiful Sanskrit verse, "Yatra yatra mano yati tatra tatra samadayaha," that means, wherever your mind goes let it go, and let it go with a deep sense of wonder. With a sense of wonderment (*Adhbhuta*), look at your mind. Among the nine *rasas* (*navarasas*) one *rasa* is called wonderment (*Adbhuta*), which Lord Krishna speaks about in the Gita. He speaks of speaking with wonder (*ashcharyavath vadathi*), looking with wonder (*ashcharyavath pashyathi*), listening with wonder (*ashcharyavath srunothi*), – everything you see is a wonder.

If you want to bring personal excellence in your life you have to get a wonderful energy from this *rasa* called *Adbhuta Rasa*. The speaker speaking is a wonder, is it not? You may say, what is the wonder, Swamiji, everybody talks. For me, speaking is such a wonder because these vocal cords are things I have not created. I am quoting a verse

15

which is automatically coming to my memory without an effort, I am keeping in mind the context of the words, and the context of the topic on personal excellence, and I am looking at this intelligent audience and this voice and in all these there is deep wonder (*adbutha*).

That I am looking at all of you is a wonder, "*ashcharyavath srunothi,*" that you are also listening is a wonder. Everything is a wonder. If you have this wonder energy with you called *Adbhuta Rasa* and with that if you look at your thoughts going up and down – what an *Adbhuta*. Without any petrol charges it is going about here and there.

What happens is you automatically start creating a harmony with a conflicting situation. Then you realise that maximum what will happen is I will not meditate, but I will lose the money, but anyway you will lose everything finally. A deep sense of wonder (*Adbhuta*) will come to you and then, the Lord says, in that *Adbhuta rasa* you start living life. Your words will then have lustre, your eyes will have lustre, every gesture is going to have lustre, there will be intelligence radiating in every part of your being. Lord Krishna in the Gita says, if you don't have this *Adbhuta*, if you don't find this energy, you will find only a dull, piles complaint energy.

I have seen some people for whom smiling means giving income tax to the Government, they can't even smile. There is no wonder (*Adbhuta*) – looking at a buffalo and looking at a Miss World, both are the same for them. But Ravindranath Tagore simply sees a dew drop on a lotus leaf and poetry comes out. This man sees Niagara Falls

16

and dysentery comes out, because he thinks water is unnecessarily wasted here, and there is no water elsewhere.

You know, some people miss the whole thrill of living and what I am saying is, this is not the right recipe, because Lord Krishna says that everything is a wonder.

So, increase your awareness and increase your silence. Learn to look at everything as a wonder. Just look – that you go to the bathroom is a wonder, that you flush is a wonder; that you drink water is a wonder, if somebody scolds you it is a wonder, if somebody fires you it is a wonder.

I say in all my workshops that you get what you focus on. Therefore, with the energy that you have for personal excellence you can bring in this *Adhbutha rasa*. How? Just by being aware. The great saint Ramana Maharishi says, "If you really enquire into your mind, you will see that there is no problematic mind – this is the direct path." (*Manasanthukim ithi margane kruthe naiva manasam ithi marga arjavath*).

This is the direct method and for that you have to increase your awareness. Not increase your knowledge – increase your awareness and as you increase your awareness, the fine-tuning you have to do is you have to be inwardly silent and inwardly calm.

In whatever you are doing, be silent and calm and you increase your awareness. When these two start happening there is a certain alchemy which happens, there is a certain synergy which happens and it is this synergy and alchemy which bring about true transformation in a person. The essence of the Gita is increase your awareness, increase

17

your inner silence, then you will create a harmony in conflict.

As long you are living you are bound to have problems. I am sure you are clear about that. If you are married there is one set of problems, not married, like me, another set of problems, having to deal with married people. If we have one wife one variety of problem, many wives, varieties of problems. If you are in India you have one set of problems. If you are Commissioner of Mumbai, one set of problems, if you are just a policeman, another set of problems. So, your problems are going to be there. Conflicts are going to be there. You have to develop the skill to be at peace with conflict. That is the message and in that peace, intelligence will come like a surf rider.

In the ocean there are waves that come and a surf rider is so aware, so relaxed, because he delicately balances when there is a wave – now he takes the surf, goes with it and as the waves come he knows how to glide through the wave and even if he falls he will fall with awareness.

He will enjoy that fall, again pick up his surf board and again he comes and goes. He enjoys the wave, which is a problem for others. He learns the art of navigating with awareness through the wave. He is also relaxed as he is doing that and he enjoys that.

But you and I are not surf riders. And every time a problem comes we grumble. You get so frustrated and you get tensed and you are not aware. The surf rider is also a human being. You are also a human being. Only thing is that he has done an exercise on living with waves so that he knows how to navigate and surf.

So too, everybody is going to face waves in life. You have to create a harmony – you will fall, everyone, you and I will fall, but we should know how to fall. Learn from your fall and go through.

Once you know this you will able to go through life in a way that is the essence of the Gita, which is that in a conflicting situation called war, Krishna is talking about peace, and for what? Not to run away from the conflicting situation but to face the conflicting situation with inner harmony.

In a conflicting situation which is war, Lord Krishna is talking about harmony, talking about peace, not to run away but face the conflicting situation like a surfer faces the waves. So too also all of us have to face waves as long as we are living. So, you are going to have problems, O Arjuna, but you should know how to navigate.

The verse says: Matra sparsastu kaunteya shitosnasukha-duhkhadah.

So the punch line is – create a harmony in conflict.

How do you create this harmony? Increase your awareness, increase the skill of being calm. Once you learn this you will be able to navigate. When you navigate you will find that, like driving, a certain skill is going to build up. As you drive you develop the skill of driving. By theorising more you will not develop and therefore, the Lord says, "Asochayan anvasochastvam pragnyavadanscha bhasase."

The 11th verse of the Chapter II of the Gita is where actual teaching (*updesha*), happens. A lot of people talk like wise persons, but they don't live as wise persons. The Lord says, "You spoke words of wisdom (*Pragyavadanshcha bhashase*), O Arjuna, you are talking words of wisdom." What was Arjuna saying? Each one feels justified in their own field. Arjuna's justification was in his conflicting situation, he felt he was in a unique position, so he was suffering uniquely. Therefore, an exception had to be made for his misery.

In my many years of counselling, I have seen that when people come and talk to me they express their problem as if it is a unique one, which nobody else in the world has. Yes, everyone is unique, hence the problem also. But the undercurrent of the problem is just the same. The undercurrent is you don't want to be a part of a solution; you want to go on justifying the problem. Effective people, even if they worry, worry effectively.

And worrying effectively means worry about whether I am part of a solution, rather than a victim to a problem. If one has to bring excellence in one's life, anywhere you have a problem, be a part of a solution. Every problem has a solution. Only, you have to learn how to look into it. If, from snake poison medicine can be created, from garbage if gobar gas can be created, if, from a rat, Walt Disney got the idea of Mickey Mouse, if all that is possible, then every problem carries in itself a certain solution.

The question is our energy. Throughout the Gita, the Lord says, we should see if our energy is focused on a solution, or we are busy justifying a problem. That justification of a problem is what He is telling Arjuna when He says, "You spoke of words of wisdom – you are talking words of wisdom, but you are not living wisely." The verse says:

"Asochayananvasochastvam praqyavadanshcha bhasase, Gatasunagatasumscha nanusochanti panditah."

Why is he just talking words of wisdom? Because Arjuna's being is in justification.

His justification is very simple. How do you expect me to fight Bhishma and Drona, he asks. How do you expect me to fight them – they are worthy of offerings of flowers, and you are telling me I have to fight my own guru, I have to fight my own grandsire, my problem is very unique. I have to fight my guru and I have to fight my own grandsire. Therefore, my position is very unique. "Katham Bhishmaham sankhye Dronam cha Madhusoodana, Ishubhihi pratiyotsyami poojarahavarisoodana."

Look into people's lives. If you work with people you will understand. Everybody starts justifying. Justification is one of the biggest obstacles in bringing about personal excellence.

In my workshop I tell people to be happy, I create humour, I make them laugh, I make them move their body differently, make them look at situations differently. And every two hours there is a break and people have to mix around after the session. And you will find the miserable looking person will look out for the other miserable person in the group, and both of them will be discussing that Swamiji says be happy, let him get married to my wife then you will see how he can be happy.

I am not joking, people have spoken like that – "It is

21

very easy to give a talk, why is he not married, tell me, and he talks on marriage; let him get married and talk." I tell you, people go on justifying. If you are in India, you will say how you can be happy in India and you want to go abroad. Now that craze has reduced a little. After going abroad, then you say, "Swamiji, whatever it may be, India is India." From there, they want to be here, and from here they want to be there. When they are alone, they say, "Swamiji I want to get married;" when they get married, somebody else is more interesting.

Here or abroad, whether you are married or not married, whether you've got good health or ill health, you are bound to be involved in problems in life. So the first thing is to be at peace with this fact, because the very fact itself can be a reason for conflict and you have a problem. And the very important teaching elaborated already is that you have to learn to create a harmony in conflict.

Really, mind cannot be happy with what is. Mind is hell. Two things happen in the mind. Many things happen, but I am highlighting two things. If you go on justifying your sorrow, that is the function of what is called *apara prakritihi*. In the 7th Chapter of the Gita, the Lord uses two terms — there is "*para prakrithi*" and "*apara prakrithi*," and in developing personal excellence, we should see this distinction. "*Apara prakrithi*" means lower nature, "*para prakrithi*" means higher nature. Lord Krishna says both these exist. He gives the description afterwards about what is the function of the lower nature (*prakrithi*).

"Bhumiraponalo vayuh kham mano buddhireva cha, ahamkara itiyam me bhinna prakrtirastadha. Apareyamitastvanyam

22

prakrtim viddhi me param, jivabhutam mahabahoyayedam dharyate jagat"

I want to highlight only one point in this verse, and that is that we go on justifying. The lower nature exists and so does the higher nature. People in whom the lower nature is dominant will go on justifying. They don't want to be a part of the solution. They want to glorify their problems. If you are a Government employee, you will justify that there is no job satisfaction. When you are in the private sector, you have excess of work.

This justifying mind should stop. And as long you are justifying, you say my problem is unique. Take up Arjuna's issue, and apply it to your own issue. Arjuna is a *kshatriya* – a warrior. A warrior is trained even to die. If you are a soldier you are willing even to die. But the only thing is death should be for a cause which should be of a very high order. If this is there, a *kshatriya*, a soldier is trained even to die. And the cause right now is – are the Kauravas rightful or wrongful in their deeds. It is very clear they are wrongful. We need not get into that deliberation.

4

DETACHMENT – AN INNER AWAKENING

"*Apara prakrithi*" means lower nature, "*para prakrithi*" means higher nature. The natural tendency of the "*apara prakrithi*" is to identify with something, and identification expresses attachment. Therefore, in the Gita the Lord says to Arjuna, be detached. "Therefore Arjuna, with a sense of detachment, continue your activities." "Tasmadasaktah satatamkaryam karma samachara."

There is a world outside and there is an inner world called "I" and "Mine." The inner world of "I" is larger than the external world. Isn't it? What is the internal world? It is nothing but your mind. The external world appears very large, but if you closely observe the internal world, your mind has got so much of "I" and "Mine," it appears larger than the external world.

For everything you say "I" and "My," so it is my book, it is my watch, my wife, my husband, then slowly you say my son – on everything you superimpose "I" and "Mine." You identify with your community, then you get identified with your subcaste; you get identified with religion, you get identified with this object or that object and this is what is called being "saktaha" in the Gita. "Sajjate" is that which sticks, so the Lord says, "tasmat asaktaha," with detachment, you start living life.

A king was suffering on account of his wife, because he was extremely attached to her. So he wanted to honour the most courageous man who was not infatuated. He called all the persons in the town and all married men were there. He said to the gathering, "Whoever is not attached to his wife, come to this side of the hall." One by one everybody started going to the other side, and soon everybody came on the other side. Only one person was left in the corner.

At last the King felt happy that in his kingdom there was this one man who was not infatuated and he said, "I am very happy, please come. I want to honour a person who is not infatuated with his wife. You are worth my 10 lakhs 'veera chakra' so please come."

The isolated man said, "Sir, please do not honour me – you see, my wife told me not to go wherever there is a crowd, and that is why I have not gone that side."

Don't take it as man and woman, but as a general statement. Please digest this. There is a world of objects, there is a world of thoughts and in the thoughts "I" and "Mine" bring so much of attachments, you go on identifying. Identification expresses attachment and throughout the Gita the Lord says to Arjuna, be detached. "Tasmat asaktaha satatam karyam karma samachara" – therefore Arjuna, with a sense of detachment continue your activities. Fight also with detachment, He says.

A surgeon has to be detached. Being detached does not mean being unconcerned. Please don't understand it wrongly. People say detached means that I should not bother. No, you be concerned. Being concerned and being worried and attached are different things altogether. If a surgeon identifies a child as his child, it is very difficult for him to do surgery. But for the neighbour's child he will do it. Not that he will be careless, but then he is not identified. When he is not identified, his effectiveness is enhanced. For your own child, you are capable of doing it, but because of the identity of "my child," "I" and "Mine," you suffer.

For example, when I am giving a talk, I should be concerned and committed in some way but I should not be attached towards the audience appreciating me or depreciating me – if you don't smile with every joke and I develop piles complaint, my effectiveness is going to go away. You observe a good sportsman when playing sports, he just focuses on the game and he is not attached to the audience, whether they are clapping or not clapping.

The natural tendency may go that way but then that is a lower nature called "*apara prakriti.*" He has to get the "*para prakriti*" and that means he has to dis-identify with the audience, focus on his game and even more, he has to focus on the moment, not even thinking of what the next game is going to be. The shot he is hitting is what he is totally focused on. When he is totally focused, in that space a different order of excellence will happen and therefore, the world of objects appears to be large but the internal world of "I" and "Mine" are larger. "I" and "Mine" are happening even in religion.

When I watch TV it is so pathetic to watch so much of lies being told. You are told to believe in this God, but you can clearly see what is happening in the name of God –

because you are attached to your religion it has to be more than the other, so believe this. I am sure all of you see this. These people are so identified with image; their only task in their life is to get a big audience. Only when they get a big audience is their food digested. And therefore, you spend so much of money, more than even in a political campaign, just to get a large audience. Why? Because they feel that they must be the largest crowd puller.

Now this lands up in identification. You cannot bring in personal effectiveness when you are identified. The message of the Gita is – don't get identified, don't get attached, not even to the result. You be focused – focus on the present right now, and when you get focused on the present without getting attached, a different order of intelligence happens.

"Karmanyevadhikaraste ma phalesu kadachana, ma karmaphalaheturbhuma te sangostvakarmani."

O Arjuna, what is happening to you right now is that you are so attached, and therefore you are justifying your attachment, and since you are justifying you are talking words of wisdom, not living it. You are weeping for things which should not be wept for. Why? Things are either dead or alive. Death is something nobody can stop. "Jathasyahe dhruvam mruthyuhu;" the Gita says, since you are born you are going to die, so why are you unhappy about death? So there is no point weeping, because death is inevitable, and for the living, you don't have to weep. So in a war either people die or win, and in either case, don't weep for them.

Elsewhere in the Gita He says, neither rejoice in success

nor in failure weep. Please understand this. Neither do you rejoice in success nor in failure do you weep, you do your duty and leave the rest to the divine. This surrender (*sharanagathi*) attitude is going to be explained in Bhakti Yoga.

The attitude that I operate from is – I will do my duty in teaching, the rest is God's blessing. If you have this type of feeling (*Bhavana*), then your craving to be successful will not exist. Here we come to a very difficult point. The Gita is going to say, be centered, be calm and be non-addictive towards both success and failure. "Siddhihi asiddhiyo samo bhootva," *siddhi*, success; *asiddhi*, failure; *samo bhootva*, be centered, be calm in both. It is one of the most beautiful teachings for personal excellence.

Management talks of how in every breakdown there is a breakthrough. I am sure all of you know this. What the Gita is talking of is more than management. Lord Krishna says in every breakthrough we also have a breakdown. Note this carefully; it is a difficult point. If you don't understand, just relax. Don't get tense about it.

Let me put it in another way. There is a failure, and in a failure you work for a success; failure is a breakdown through which you get a breakthrough. All management systems say – convert every breakdown into a breakthrough.

The Gita is talking of more than that. It says your success can be the greatest failure in your life. When a person who has become highly successful has to leave all his success behind at the time of death that will be the greatest failure.

29

So unless you are enlightened, even your success can become the greatest failure. Therefore, the message is that the very success becomes a failure because either some other competitor can beat this achiever or if he is at the top at the time of his death, he has to drop his success and the soul has to go, and in that he has the experience of his failure because all he has done is invest in a sinking ship.

Therefore, Lord Krishna says, when you become successful, somebody else can beat you, so success itself is a failure, which is one thing. Or at the time of death, all you have invested is in the bubble, the bubble is going to burst and you have to leave your investment, so at that time it is a failure, so what should you do. So, don't get entrapped in failure, don't get entrapped in success.

It means your happiness should not be confined by failure, and your happiness should not be defined by success either. At present our happiness is defined by our success and confined by our failure, our happiness is entrapped by our success or failure.

You can set happiness, for example, in a space like a hall, so it is limited by this hall; but if you see it from another angle this space is not limited by this hall because in fact the hall exists in the space. If you look within the angle of the hall, it appears space is in the hall; but if look from the angle of space, the hall is in space. So too, your consciousness is Chidambaram, Chidakashaha. There is a center in you that is tremendously pure, your failure cannot entrap it and your success cannot define it. Your happiness is defined neither by success nor failure. Can we set ourselves free like this?

That is why in Yoga, after doing all asanas, at the end you do shavasan. Ultimately, whatever asanas you do, you have to leave this world. When you are free to see when living itself that the body is dead, that means your life is not entrapped by the movement of the body. If you can get that space that Lord Krishna is unfolding, happiness is not confined by failure, neither is it defined by success.

"Gatasunagatasumsca nanusochanti panditah," meaning the wise person, "panditaha," grieves not, "na anushochanti."

That is why Sartre said hell is other people. Why did he say that? For ordinary people, happiness is invariably defined by others' statements. If somebody praises you, you are happy, if somebody criticises you, you are in a breakdown. Our happiness, our sorrow is dependant upon the other's praise and criticism. So hell is other people.

Lord Krishna says – don't let your life depend on success or failure. Life is just a movement from moment to moment. Your mind with ignorance says, life is happy if I get this, and life is unhappy if I don't get this.

This interpretation of the mind messes up the wonderful movement of life. If you can set this movement free, life becomes indeed beautiful. Through yoga of knowledge (*jnana yoga*) Lord Krishna is trying to convey this, and some of you can understand what I am saying. For some of you it goes above your head.

So then Lord Krishna says – just pray for the Lord's blessings, just learn to pray, to say, O Lord, by your blessings, the impossible is possible because there is an alchemy which can bless and transform. "Mookam karoti vachalam, Pangum langhyate girim," it is said, which means that the Lord can bless the dumb with speech and make the lame climb the mountain.

If you cannot follow Gnana yoga, if you pray with Bhakti, mystical blessings can also transform your life, and that becomes the yoga of devotion *(Bhakti yoga)*. You can offer a leaf *(patram)*, a flower *(pushpam)*, a fruit *(phalam)* or even water *(toyam)*, but offer it with Bhakti.

The verse says: "Patram pushpam phalam toyam, yo ma bhaktya prayachhati."

Just close your eyes, and full of devotion, open your heart and seek the blessings of the lord. Let your mind get dissolved in devotion. Feel the lord's blessings in you.

5

COMMITMENT – THE
AWAKENING OF EXCELLENCE

There is a very beautiful Sanskrit saying, spoken by a Rishi, which goes that if water falls on a hot pan, instantly, it gets burnt away. When water falls on a lotus leaf, the lotus becomes more beautiful with the dancing of a dewdrop of water, but with a little breeze the water will disappear. But if the same water falls on an oyster, it takes that one dewdrop of water and converts it into a pearl.

For some people, listening to the teachings is like water falling on a dosa pan, as you listen it disappears. If you are filled with anger, jealously, hatred, upsetness, your mind is like the dosa pan, and the teachings of the Gita can be like beautiful water, but as it falls it disappears.

A little more evolved person is a lotus and the teaching is like water falling on a lotus flower. With this dewdrop the lotus is more beautiful. But the moment you go home, your wife says, "Idiot, why have you come late," and all the teaching goes away like the dewdrop disappearing with the breeze.

But if you are like an oyster, and keep the water, then the same water will turn into a pearl. So too the teachings of

Gita... like the water described above, and you can choose to be a dosa pan, or a lotus flower, or an oyster.

And what is required if your life has to get transformed into one of personal excellence, is that you should be like an oyster. When you listen to the Gita from a deep commitment, you will keep the teaching and it will turn into a pearl.

Vyavasayatmika buddhirekeha kurunandana
Bahushakha hyanantasca buddhayovyavasayinam.

Lord Krishna in the Gita says that your life should have the quality of single pointedness (*vyvasayatmika buddhirekhe*), and your mind should not be loaded with desires (*bahushakha*), because such a mind is not integrated, and it is easily shattered. Such a person may listen to the best of teachings from the greatest of masters and yet it will not bless him.

The great author Sankarananda says that if you want enlightenment, you should focus intensely on it and say I want enlightenment, and enlightenment alone – "Eshwaraha eva asmaham paragatihi." In the same way, if you want to transform your life through personal excellence, and with that focus and commitment you start listening, a different quality will open up.

So you have to make a decision – can I be focused? Can I be centered?

It is like a musical note or a raga. You should have the maturity to understand it, and to get that you should have commitment. It is the same thing with the Bhagavad Gita. The person whose mind is not evolved, he just listens from one ear and lets it go from the other. But if you can really listen to the Gita you will find each verse loaded with meaning.

When a fruit is given you should not see just the outer layer, you should see the diamond hidden in the fruit. And only when you see that diamond, will awakening happen.

Speaking of diamonds, there is a beautiful Sufi story - a person goes to a Sufi master and says, "O Master, will you teach me spirituality?" And the master says, "I will teach you, but before that, take this stone, and don't sell it, but go and find out its worth and come back." The story goes that the man takes it to a vegetable vendor, who says it is worth one rupee, and then he goes to a silversmith, who says it is worth Rs. 1000. He reports this to the master, who says, "Now, go to the goldsmith and find out."

The goldsmith puts its value at Rs. 1 lakh, and the student is very excited, but the master tells him to show it to a diamond merchant. That man says, "I will give you Rs. 15 lakh." Again he comes back all excited, and the master says, "Please understand that this is worth Rs. 30 crore. None of these people know it, they interpret according to their ability. This is a diamond worth 30 crores."

Hence, in the Gita the Lord says, "Nahi gnanena sadrisham pavithramiha vidyate;" there is nothing more purifying than right understanding and if you don't have the right understanding, your intellect is clouded with ignorance, and you live your life in delusion. "Agnanenavritham gnanam tena muhyanti jantavaha." When ignorance (*agnana*) covers the intellect, your life is a deluded one (*muhyanti*).

6

THE THREE REALITIES – FROM PRISON TO DIVINE PRESENCE

I t is a very important verse in the Gita, where the Lord says the cause of miseries in our lives is not our situation in life. Most of us think we are suffering in life because of the "sandarbha," the situation in life – people say, I am suffering, Swamiji, because of this situation, I am suffering because of that situation and everyone starts justifying the situation, saying I am poor, so I am unhappy, or I am rich therefore I am unhappy, because I am worrying about the income tax officers or the terrorists who will kidnap me.

So everybody goes on justifying the situation, but it is really not the situation that causes suffering. The teaching of the Gita is that more than the situation, the "sandarbha," it is your internal state that either gives you your sorrow or does not.

The Lord says, your intellect is covered with ignorance. "Agnanena avritam gnanam." When it is covered with ignorance, it is this ignorance you are basically suffering from. Your situation has one unit of impact, but your inability to face the situation, because of ignorance, has a deeper impact on your life.

Therefore, to raise a person's excellence, his understanding has to be raised. If you want to be personally effective in life, you have to understand whether it is the situation which is killing your life, and making it miserable, or is it your ability or inability to face the situation which is giving you chaos. It is an important discrimination (*viveka*) we should have in life, otherwise we generally we blame our misery on a situation.

I will convey this with an example. An elderly man and a youngster are seated in a bar having a dialogue. Another youngster comes in and before even taking his drink, he just sits down and starts overhearing the conversation.

The elderly man asks the youngster, "Where do you live?" And the youngster says, "I live in B2, Anand Apartments, in Rajmahal Vilas Extension, Bangalore." And the elderly man says, "My God, I also live in the same apartment. How is that we have not met?" Then the elderly person asks the youngster, "How long have you been living there?" He says, "For 25 years." And the elderly man says, "My God, 25 years I have been living there and how is it that we have not met?"

Now the person listening to that was utterly confused. He had not even started his drink and he hears two people say they have lived for 25 years in the same area, same flat, same floor and both say they have not seen each other.

A bar attender, who was passing that side, gently tapped the new person and said,"Sir, don't get confused. These two people, the elderly man and the youngster, come every night, get drunk, and have the same conversation – where do you live, which flat? How many years? They are nothing but father and son."

In a drunken state, the deep connection between the father and the son is not seen by either. The Lord says we are unhappy because we are also drunk. We are drunk with what? With an alcohol called ignorance. We are drunk with the alcohol called ignorance and we are not able to see that the happiness we are searching for is right within our own senses. The unhappiness that we experience is not because of the situations in life, but because the mind deals with the situation in such a way that we are unhappy. Unhappiness is not in the situation; it is the state of being that you are in.

Therefore, for personal effectiveness, ask yourself this question. Is the situation disturbing you? Or is it how you are looking at the situation which is disturbing you? If you are looking at it with ignorance, then that ignorance is what is really disturbing you.

Hence philosophy in Sanskrit is called "Darshan Sastra," because "darshan" means seeing. Can you see, right now, that first there is an external reality, which is one situation, and there is another situation called the internal reality, which is your interpretation in your mind?

Your soliloquy is your likes and your dislikes, it is your dogma and your opinion, it is your judgement and your preconceived notion, it is the internal dialogue which is the internal reality. A gross person sees only the external reality – for example, you see this chair I am sitting on. After I get up and go, you still see this chair, and the external reality is this chair that you see.

Now somebody else looks at this same chair and says, "My Master has sat on it and given a talk on the Bhagavad

Gita, my father also sat on the same chair, my mother also sat on the same chair." And the same chair is viewed with tremendous respect, tremendous reverence. Now the respect and reverence do not make him see the chair as the chair, and the chair becomes the object of devotion. Now, is that the external reality or internal reality? It becomes an internal reality.

So, there is an external reality and there is also an internal reality of your mind. Throughout the Gita the Lord goes on saying that this internal reality of your mind, if it is not properly purified, and you look at the external reality, or object, from the polluted state of being, then your perception of the object is that the object is the source of your chaos.

But the object is actually not the cause of the chaos, it is the internal reality that is interpreting the external reality that is the cause, and so life becomes a mixed reality, a combination of external reality and internal reality.

Without much quoting of slokas there, I want you to see the essence for your personal excellence. Once you purify your internal state, then what happens is that when you perceive an object, you see an object as an object, and then you see that the real tension that comes is not in the object, it is in your mind that is interpreting the object.

For example, you are invited to a party. You dress up very well. You have gone into a party in a five-star atmosphere, a beautiful five-star atmosphere. Once in the party, you see beautiful crockery on the table, then you see people wearing diamond rings, people with beautiful shoes, then you look at all of them and say, "My God, she is wearing a diamond earring, my useless husband has given me only gold earrings. She is wearing a wonderful nose ring. My useless husband he says that a nose is enough, ring is not at all required." So what has happened? Somebody is wearing a diamond ring, and nose rings are wonderful things to be observed. But you don't see the diamond rings, the beautiful crockery on the table – you don't see all that. What you say is, "I do not have, somebody has." Somebody having a diamond earring becomes a whipping point for you that you do not have it.

Now, the external reality is beautiful crockery, beautiful ambience and beautiful diamonds people are wearing. Is that impacting you, or is it your internal reality which says, "I do not have the diamond ring, I do not have this diamond necklace," which is impacting you more? It is this internal reality, which is creating inner chaos.

Therefore, although the external reality has a unit of impact, the internal reality has a deeper unit of impact. You have to become alert towards this. Therefore Saint Kabir says, "manke har har hai manke jit jit." If mind says "har gaya," you have lost. If it says "jit," you've won. This is referring to internal reality.

Now there is a third level of reality which is called transcendental reality.

So we have the external reality, the internal reality, then the transcendental reality and in that transcendental reality, you can discover another space. It is like space being present in a hall and this hall also being present in a space. The space (akasha) is in this hall, the hall is also in space. Call it the "hall space" – when you break the hall, the hall space does not exist, but space exists. There is a pot, there is a space in the pot, it is "ghatakashaha." Now it appears that the space in the pot is limited by the pot. But if you look at the transcendental reality, the pot exists in space. So if you break the pot, pot space is destroyed ... but space is not destroyed. This reality is called transcendental reality. "Ghataha tasmin ghate akashaha vartate ataha dehakashaha."

In the same way the Gita says consciousness exists in the body like space exists in a hall. You are aware only of this reality. So you feel consciousness is entrapped in the body, but the Lord says, the body exists in consciousness. When the body is destroyed it appears that consciousness is destroyed, just as when the pot is destroyed it appears pot space is destroyed. Yes, the pot space is destroyed but space itself is not destroyed.

Therefore, when the body is destroyed consciousness is not destroyed. Consciousness in the body is destroyed. But then the body exists in consciousness. This reality is called the transcendental reality.

In developing personal excellence you must understand this fact very clearly. There is an external reality which has one unit of impact, we are not negating that, but more real than the external reality is the internal reality – when your mind interprets something as sorrow, it is sorrow. If the mind does not interpret it as sorrow, it is not sorrow.

Therefore the mental state is more real than the external state. To that extent you say the world is unreal. Not that the world is unreal, but when your mind gains a deeper reality, from that space we say the world is unreal.

Take a deep breath. You will understand this better with

more oxygen in the brain. Now you understand there is another level of reality, into which the Lord inviting us to get into, and it is called transcendental reality. It appears to you that you have understood, but you have not understood it, because nothing is happening. That is because that apparatus which has to understand it has to go through purification.

And Lord Krishna in the Gita says, if it is not purified, then you will understand but the understanding has to reach a peak before it becomes wisdom. Water boils at 100 degrees. If it stops at 99 degrees, the water is not going to boil. The water is hot, but it is not boiled. This is what exactly happens when your understanding has come to a level, but it has yet to reach 100 degrees, where the knowledge transforms into wisdom. Only then it is a blessing.

But what happens is we do not have patience to wait until that. When the water comes to 99 degrees we think, "Oh, it is not boiling," and switch it off. When you switch it off, you have to start once again. Your understanding has to come to a boiling point and then it becomes wisdom. Then your knowledge clicks. The knowledge that clicks is called wisdom.

In personal excellence you have to understand this. Like when somebody cracks a joke, everybody laughs but I am a tube light, I do not laugh. I understand the grammar of the joke, I understand everything of the joke, but it does not click. Like some of you understood now, there is a transcendental reality, but it is not clicking.

So when a joke is cracked, everybody laughs. I

understand the joke, the joke does not click at that time. But I go on reflecting on the joke, and after five days, in the bathroom, ah, it clicks now. Generally in the bathroom it clicks because everything is released, and so ignorance is also released. I have earlier understood the joke, but the joke has clicked now, and the real blessing of the joke is when the joke clicks. I am putting a complex Vedantic truth in a simple way to make you understand.

So you know that there is an external reality, you know there is an internal reality, you know that there is a transcendental reality. You understand consciousness is not in the body, but the body exists in consciousness, but it is not clicking, because water has to reach 100 degrees for it to boil. Until that point you need a commitment. And if you don't bring in your commitment it will all just disappear.

That transcendental reality is what the Lord talks about in the 12th verse of Chapter II, when he tells Arjuna:

Natvevaham jatu nasam na tvam neme janadhipah
Na chaiva na bhavisyamah sarve vayamatah param.

It is not as though neither you, nor I, nor these kings have never existed before; nor is it that we shall cease to exist in the future.

The quintessence of this verse is, "O Arjuna, you have existed before your birth and you will exist after your death. The kings who are standing in front of you existed before their birth they will also exist after their death." It means there is a centre in you which is unaffected by your birth, there is a centre in you which is unaffected by death.

The point is, even if you have to worry, you have to worry effectively. Here the Lord explains why you should not worry. He says there is a centre in us, which is very pure, which is eternal, which is permanent, which is what I referred to as a transcendental reality, in Sanskrit it is called "paramatmika tatvam." There is such a centre in us, but we are looking only the periphery of ourselves, we are not looking at the core.

This is the important teaching of the Gita. Are you looking superficially or are you looking very deeply? An artist, when he has to paint a flower, looks at the same flower many times, and if you ask him, and he is sincere in replying, he will say the same flower speaks to him in different ways. When he looks at the same flower, he looks afresh each time, looks deeply, and every turn, every colour, every element of the flower is going to be very different; it is just not a flower, it is ecstasy which is dancing which he has to capture in his painting. But when the gross person looks at the flower, he finds only the flower. So the gaze of an artist, the painter of a flower is very different from that of an ordinary person when he looks at a flower.

So too the Lord says, in your search for personal excellence, when you look at an issue, look at your own self more deeply. We are all busy looking at the world, we are not busy looking at ourselves. Therefore Veda beautifully says that we are all looking outward, we have never taken time to look inward.

If you don't understand relax. Don't create a conflict by worrying, especially if you are a Hindu, because you have many births apart from this one. So just relax, because only in a state of relaxation will something happen.

As the Zen expression goes, do nothing when spring comes, and the grass will grow by itself. Doing nothing means don't go on worrying. Worrying is the greatest activity people have. For everything they will worry.

One person came to me and said, "Swamiji, I have seen many people doing your workshop, all are very happy, and as for me I have no problem. Other people have wife problem, husband problem, stepney problem, but I have no problem, except one, Swamiji – who I was in my previous birth? With a little Buddhist background, I have gone through many of your books, and there is a technique, which tells you who you were in the previous birth. Please tell me, Swamiji who I was. This is the only tension I have."

I said, "Why do you want to know who you were in the previous birth?" He said, "Please don't say all that, Swamiji. Give me a technique." I said, "I will give you a technique and you may realise that in the previous birth you were a rat. If Buddha was an elephant you were a rat. And if you realise you were a rat by a certain technique, then what will happen?

You cannot live in your previous birth, you have to come back to your present birth. And in the present birth if you live in the last one, what will happen? You will see a rat in your house going up and down, and you may see this as your grandchild. So you will have a new problem now. You will say you cannot sleep with the grandchildren running around, and the wife will say, "Why, who are you sleeping with?" You will enter into lot of complications."

Therefore, in the 15th Chapter of the Gita the Lord says,

I am forgetfulness. Even forgetfulness is my glory. If all of us remember who we were in the previous birth, this knowledge of who we were then will become an unnecessary burden. So, stop worrying ineffectively. If you understand this right now, well and good, if you don't understand, again, well and good.

Therefore, the Lord says all of us existed before our birth and all of us will exist after our death. The space existed before the pot, the space exists when you break the pot and the pot space dies, but the space exists after the pot space dies. The space of the consciousness is the Chidambaram, the Chidakashaha, it exists before the body and it exists also after the body.

Therefore, there is a centre in us, which is absolute, there is a centre in us which is permanent, because the very fact that death is happening means there is something deathless from which the phenomena of death can happen. If there is knowledge, there must be ignorance. If there is black, then there must be white. The opposite must exist. If there is change, there must be something changeless. Or else, how will you discover change. Something changing is recognised only against the backdrop of something which is changeless. Therefore, the Lord is saying, look at that changeless principle. O Arjuna, there is a centre in us which is unpolluted, there is a centre in us which is a purity. Therefore even in the Bible it is said that there is a childlike nature in us. You have to discover that, but you are looking at the periphery and not looking at the centre.

In your search for your personal excellence also you arrive at a pure centre within you, because there is a centre of purity within us. You are not able to see that centre which is eternal. It is in that centre which is eternal that the phenomenon of change is constantly happening.

You may not understand this, but still you've got it. This is what happens in life. So often you get it and still you have not got it. I will give some symbols for you to understand the essence of the Gita. One of the biggest symbols of the Gita is of a person who is in deep sleep, and the trumpets are blowing and the drums are beating and still this man is snoring.

And there is a divine ladder from the earth to heaven that can be climbed, so trumpets and drums are playing loudly to wake up the sleeper, but still he is sleeping. The teaching of this symbol is that we are all asleep, and the Gita is like a divine ladder, which tells you climb from worldly living to divine living.

The ladder is there, you only need to climb it, but you are not doing so because you are asleep. And in fact, every moment, Krishna, Buddha, Rama and all the great mahatmas are blowing the conches, they are blowing their trumpets telling us to wake up, but still we are snoring.

Why is it like this? I will give you another symbol to explain that. Let us say this sleeping person gets up and he is in prison and it is locked. He has been living in the prison for so long, he has become comfortable with it.

Somebody, for example a master, a guru, comes to him and gives him a key and says that with this key he can open the prison gate and go out. He takes the key, respects the master, but he says I am very comfortable in my prison, so I will not use the key. He has got so used to prison habits, even though the key is given to him to go out of the prison, he is not going out of it. The prison habits have gone so deep within. This is the picture Lord Krishna is drawing for us. If you feel personal excellence has to happen, you have to come out of this prison. And there are many prisons; the body itself becomes a prison to people. If you only look at yourself as body and don't even realise that you have a mind, the body can become a prison. So also, the emotion itself becomes a prison, or the mind itself becomes a prison to people. The whole message of the Gita is, transform the prison into a presence.

Body, emotions, mind, being – each can become a prison. For example, a person came to the Krishna temple in my ashram. He bowed down to Lord Krishna. I saw that as he was bowing down he was looking at his body. He is a body builder, actually. So when he does "archana" he sees which muscle is working. He is so body conscious that the body, instead of being a ladder for him to discover something which is beyond itself, has been converted into a prison. And then he develops prison habits.

So too, emotions are extremely wonderful. But if you don't purify your emotions through Bhakti yoga, they too can become a prison. Your mind can become a prison if you don't purify it; the process of purification of mind is called yoga of knowledge, Gnana yoga. To purify your emotions is Bhakti yoga. For purifying your being there is Dhyana yoga. And to purify body consciousness, so that you can go to the mind, there is Hatha Yoga. In this way, through yoga, a prison can become a presence. When your prison becomes a presence, it is no more the obstacle.

7

YOGA – THE ART OF DROPPING PRISON HABITS

here are four important yogas in the Gita – Gnana, Bhakti, Karma, and Dhyana. Gnana yoga is about understanding, Bhakti yoga is about devotion, and in the Bhakti yoga, there are three types: shravana bhakti, listening is called shravana bhakti; sankeertana bhakti, which refers to repeating a chant, and experiencing a certain joy in your chanting itself; and the third is called smarana bhakti, which means just remembering the Lord.

That is why, when there is a bhajan I want everybody to take part in it. "Satatam keertayanto ma" – Lord Krishna says, always (*satatam*) try to glorify me, (*keertayanto ma*), and once you start doing that, you will develop a certain acumen, a certain acuity and you start seeing the not-ordinary. Like in management you say out of the box thinking, you start seeing something very extraordinary in the so-called ordinary.

In a seed there is an infinite capacity to grow. Infinity exists in the finite seed. A seed planted becomes a tree. From a tree again there is a fruit, from a fruit a seed, from a seed a tree, so in a finite seed there is the infinite capacity to grow.

Therefore, that acumen, to look at something divine in the very ordinary, develops. Vikramaditya's master showed how a fruit may look like a gross fruit but inside there is something divine. That apparatus to see – this is what you get by Gnana yoga and by Bhakti yoga. There is also the way of Karma yoga and Dhyana yoga and also Hatha yoga. When you build that acumen through yoga, then a different level of personal excellence can readily flow into different walks of your life.

Karma yoga, Bhakti yoga, Gnana yoga and Dhyana yoga–this is the whole quintessence. It is simple that everybody understands it, yet, something does not click.

I will explain why through a simple mudra called "surabhi" used in the sandhyavandana – a vedic ritual and prayer. Surabhi means the udder of the cow. If you squeeze the teats of the udder, milk will flow. Milk is in the cow. But it comes through the udder. So you should know how to milk it.

The mudra called "surabhi" is this important concept and that becomes, in a way, the summary of the whole Gita, which means that if you take the understanding to 100 degrees boiling point, only then it clicks. If you understand this, you understand the gist of the Gita.

There is in us a body centre, an emotional centre, and an intellectual centre. These become prisons to us because of lack of understanding. We have to turn each into a presence. In this body centre, emotional centre, intellectual centre, purification happens through Karma yoga, Hatha yoga, Bhakti yoga, Gnana yoga.

Your intellectual centre can be mechanical, or it can be

magnetic. Your intellectual centre can be used for mechanical thinking. If you listen to the Gita with mechanical thinking, then it is like the best of seeds sown in infertile soil – nothing is going to click. So for your personal excellence, your intellect has to go through what is called a ·Gnana yoga discipline.

Gnana means understanding, yoga means to join. You have to join yourself to understanding and then purification happens. If whatever I am saying falls in the mechanical centre of your buddhi, your intellect, you will understand it only superficially.

I will give you an example of how the mechanical center works. Lots of people use religion very mechanically and, instead of a means of growth, religion becomes a stumbling block for such people.

There is a story about a fanatic Jew (but don't take it seriously about him being a Jew, it's a story). Some fanatic Jew in Israel gave an offer, that for every Palestinian you are going to kill, you are going to get 1000 dollars. So two Jews took their guns and said, "Let us go to Palestine." They went and searched for Palestinians, but in vain.

They got tired and slept. After a while one Jew awoke and shook the other Jew, saying, "Get up, get up, we are going to become very rich!" The other fellow opened his eyes, and saw around them 200 Palestinians with guns.

He also started calculating, so these two were using their intellects, but mechanically, being hooked to money, money, and money. This is using your intellect mechanically. And with such a mechanical mind even if you listen to a Gita discourse, you listen to see if it is fitting in with your convictions of how the Gita should be.

You listen from that angle, and not from an angle of, "Hey, am I learning how to transform myself?" For this to happen, an intellect that is a mechanical center should become a magnetic centre. When your intellect becomes a magnetic centre, your understanding will be deep and not superficial.

One student tells the other student, "Hey, my Guru performs these miracles. What does your guru perform?" To which this man says, "In your world, if God fulfils your will it is a miracle. But in my world; if we fulfill God's will, that is a miracle." Two totally different kinds of understanding are here, side by side.

Through Gnana yoga your intellect is changing from the mechanical centre into the magnetic centre. In Sanskrit it is called Jeevatma to Paramatma. But in Bhakti yoga too, the emotional centre can be extremely mechanical. Have you seen people whose emotions are very mechanical? They look at somebody and a certain strong emotion gets switched on. And often, that emotion has no basis even. For example, I was in somebody's farm, and a person next to me said, "If I look at that bird, it irritates Swamiji." Now, the fact was that I was not irritated – in fact, I love birds. But that person had a strong feeling which just got switched on. That is what I call a mechanical emotion centre. Like a machine it starts working in a person's life.

There was a Pathan about to get married. Another Pathan said to him, "Take my advice, all my grey hair is not only knowledge but wisdom. Right from the first day, you should control your wife. Ladies appear to be weak but they are super strong. Most men are henpecked but pretend to be men.

So right from first day, if you are not strict, look at my plight, you will also be like this." This fellow has to follow the advice of elders.

He gets married the next day. From the first night, this tall Pathan tells his wife, "You know who I am, I'm a Pathan. Four o'clock in the morning, I want hot water or else …!" he screams. This lady shivers. Every night before going to sleep he says, "Tomorrow, hot water or else …!"

Ten years go by, nine children have been produced and the tenth is on the way. He has turned the wife into an industry to produce children. She gets so fed up, finally, one day when he says, "Tomorrow, hot water or else…!" the wife musters so much of courage that she asks, "Or else what will you do?" "I will take a cold water bath," he says. The basic emotion of this man is fear.

The point I'm making is that you have to identify your core weakness, so that you move from the mechanical emotional centre to the magnetic emotional centre. Through Bhakti yoga your mechanical emotion should become a magnetic center.

One of the best examples is in the life history of Vachaspathi Mishra, one of the greatest saints who wrote wonderful commentaries on very difficult texts called Brahmasutras. It took him many years and finally, he finished his commentary. He raised his head, and he found an old lady with a lantern at his door who came in with his food. And this man asked, "Who are you?"

And she said, "For the last twenty years you have been

writing these commentaries, so you have forgotten me – I am your wife. I knew you were contributing something tremendously important to humanity by writing commentaries on the Brahmasutras written by Veda Vyasa. So I did not want to disturb you at all. Every night I would just come and leave food, and so you are not able to recognise me. But I am happy you have completed the work."

When he heard this sacrifice of his wife for 20 years, tears flowed. He said, "I have no words to thank you for your sacrifice. I could not recognise my own wife. But I am in conflict now."

Vachaspathi Mishra, who wrote great commentaries, is in conflict. "What is the conflict?" asked his wife. "I had taken a vow that if I finish the text I am going to take sanyas. Now that I see this sacrifice of yours of 20 years that you have come and served me, I am in conflict about whether to respect your sacrifice or to honour my words."

So she said, "The very tears you have in your eyes is enough proof that you love me and you care for me, so continue in your commitment." Then, this great saint named the book of commentaries on Brahmasutras as Bhamati, because that was the name of his wife. Very few people know that the author of the book is Vachaspathi Mishra, because the book is called Bhamati.

The ordinary person who listens to this story may feel this is foolish, it is madness, but once the emotion reaches the peak, it is like mother who does so much to the children, the giving itself is joy without receiving. So when you bring the emotion to the peak the giving has such a beauty, more even than receiving, and then your emotion has become a magnetic centre.

Through Bhakti yoga your mechanical emotions transform into a magnetic centre. Through Gnana yoga your buddhi, your intellect transforms from a mechanical centre to a magnetic centre. Through the principle of Hatha yoga and Karma yoga mechanical body movements become magnetic. That is when transformation really happens. This body, which is mechanical, has become a prison, because we develop prison habits, and that which is mechanical has to become magnetic – this is the quintessence of Gita.

The body should become a magnetic center. For example, if I am talking to you, my hand gestures should be relaxed. If I make my gestures with a lot of tension that is the mechanical centre.

Therefore, in yoga, asana is called "sthira sukham asanam." "Sthiram" means you have to be firm, "sukha" means you have to be relaxed and "sukha" also means you have to be happy. So as I talk I have to be relaxed, at the same time I have to be happy. When that happens this body centre becomes a magnetic center, it opens up magnetically.

Be aware of the way you perceive life. When you take a bath, feel the water is a divine feel the sunrise is a "devata," see the flora and fauna, the stars in the sky as divine blessings.

The Upanishad says: "Eshavasyam idam sarvam" – everything is divine. For some other person the same sun rising at 6 o'clock and the birds singing disturb his sleep, but the same birds chirping can be a divine experience, a divine song if the same ears hear from the magnetic centre of the body.

For mechanical persons the birds singing can be a great nuisance. Therefore, the discipline of yoga is to purify this body, which the Lord explains as "Yuktahara viharasya," meaning your eating (*ahaara*), and the entertainments of the body (*vihara*) have to be moderate and balanced. When you do so there is a sensory acuity, a sensory sharpness that opens up and then you perceive the world very differently.

A Westerner came to India to learn Indian archery. In Indian archery, the master talks less, and communicates through silence. In India, we believe in "mouna vyakhya prakatita parabrahma tatvam yuvanam," as Adi Sankaracharya says, which means that through silence, the master conveys more than through words.

So when the Westerner came to learn Indian archery the master said, "Observe me and learn." The master takes the bow and arrow and takes aim and releases the arrow, and hits the bull's eye.

Now this man observes the stance of the guru, he also takes the bow and arrow and shoots, but misses the target. And the master says, "Every day, observe the posture which I am taking, learn it and repeat it."

Every day this man goes on doing this and every time it misses, but the guru hits the target. One day he hits the bull's eye. He feels very happy that he has learnt Indian archery. He rushes to his master, touches his feet and says, "I have learnt Indian archery."

The master says, "Show me." He takes the bow and arrow and focuses. Before he shoots, the master says, "You missed the target." This man gets confused, thinking, "I have not even shot the arrow, how can I miss the target."

And the master says, "Observe me and then do accordingly," and goes away. Next day he observes how he hits the target. The student takes aim but before he shoots, the master says, "You missed the target."

The student gets so confused that he packs his bags and says, "Indian gurus are the most dangerous people; A Westerner has written a book titled "Hunting for a Guru." At the end of the book he says that he could not find a guru, though he hunted for one. I would have told him that because gurus are intelligent in India, if you hunt for one, all of them will run away.

A guru is not to be hunted; he has to be invited.

So anyway, this man got so frustrated that he packed his bags and started to leave, but suddenly some sanity, some pure centre within him awakened and said, "Hey, my master does not appear to be insane, there must be some message he is trying to convey," and with this he logged on to the pure centre within himself and then he had the "shraddha" to see what it was all about.

So, as the master was picking up his bow and arrow in his morning practice, suddenly enlightenment dawned on the Westerner. He came rushing to the master and touched his feet, and said, "I have learnt Indian archery." He said, "Show it." He picked up the bow and arrow, as he took aim, the master said, "Yes, you have learnt Indian archery." And he released the arrow and hit the bull's eye.

What this man learnt is that the first time when he hit the target properly, he was holding the bow with tension and with anxiety; therefore, even though he hit the target, the way he hit the target was not Indian archery, not Zen archery.

So the man realised that hitting the target is not all that is important, but the way you hit the target and how relaxed you are, how calm you are, how focused you are without worrying about the result, is important, and keeping the body in that state that is called the magnetic center is important.

When he realised it, he picked up the bow and arrow in such a relaxed manner and took such a relaxed posture that the master said, "You have learnt Indian archery."

How restless we are when we move our body, even while just scratching the head. Restlessly scratching the head means the body is being mechanical – scratching at nothing on top of the head, and there is nothing inside either.

Have you seen some people eating food? They press the rice in such a way that it appears they are fighting with food, with rice particles going in all parts of the fist. Eating food is called Annapoorneshwari Upasanam in Indian tradition. Eating the food itself is a meditative act, your eating the food should be relaxed.

So the body should be very relaxed, and at the same time happy. Some people say, "I am very happy, Swamiji... very relaxed." It is like sugarcane with the juice all squeezed, there is no essence at all. This happiness is like the graveyard's silence. So the body should be relaxed, and the body should be happy. "Sthiram sukham asanam" –

"*sukha*" means relaxed and happy.

When these two disciplines are there, the magnetic centre of the body opens up. That is why if you are doing yogasanas, you are keeping your body pure. Even your sexual act becomes very pure and sacred. Convert "*maithuna*" (the sexual act) into "*prarthana*" (prayer), says the Kamasutra. Even your sexual act should be a prayer. If you keep your body centre like that you find in yourself a sensory sharpness.

In psychology it is called sensory acuity. If you are giving a talk you can sense whether the audience is understanding or not understanding. As a businessman you will be able to sense whether the customer is interested in this product or not interested in it. And therefore, such sensory sharpness is important for your personal excellence.

The sixth sense should be there, even in business. If you are doing yoga, you are living a pure and clean life – your sexual act is clean, your eating habits are clean, your moving habits are clean – so then there is a magnetic centre which opens up. So the body can intuit and for business and for personal excellence, sometimes you should know how to sense a person.

As a policemen also you have to be intuitive. I asked a policeman, "How do you find out who is smuggling?" He said, "Very simple, Swamiji. We can sense if a person is a smuggler or not. Most of the times our guesses are very correct. Usually, they are restless. Some people pose as if they are very calm. But we are able to guess they are not." This is sensory sharpness.

As a part of personal excellence, you should also know

61

who is interested in you. Some people just don't know that.

One student came to me, and started massaging my leg, and said, "Swamiji, I love you very much." "What happened, what do you want?," I asked. "Swamiji, I am deeply in love with one of your students." So he wants me to do courier work, I thought. Such is the status of a Swamiji in Kaliyuga. I understand why some gurus keep away from students.

He said, "I am also your student, please help me Swamiji. If Lord Krishna could help Arjuna to elope with his own sister, why cannot you do it for me, Swamiji?" Now he quotes scripture also.

I know this man is a good person, very innocent at heart. I also knew the student he was in love with, so I told the student the next day when she came to my ashram about his love. She said, "That idiot, you want me to get married to him, Swamiji?" I was shocked because that person was so intelligent and highly qualified. "Why are you calling him an idiot?" I asked her.

She said, "For the past five years I've been giving signals to the idiot that I am interested, and still he cannot get it." You see how poor his sensory sharpness was.

This incident opened my heart to understanding things much better. I am sure if Lord Krishna comes now, not in a regular form but in jeans, none of us will recognise him. Because we are so arrogant, we decide how Krishna should be dressed.

If the Buddha comes wearing shorts and a monkey cap, none of the Buddhists will recognise him, because we have such preconceived opinions about how he should be dressed.

And therefore we cannot see through the outer layer of people. I have seen people so evolved who are not even monks. I have seen so many monks who can talk so much knowledge but are not at all evolved.

It is this sensory sharpness one should have and when that happens, the magnetic centre of the body opens up – the magnetic centre, not the mechanical centre. Through the practice of yoga, when this magnetic centre opens up in different areas – in the intellect through Gnana yoga, in the emotions through Bhakti yoga, in the body through Hatha yoga and Karma yoga – when all these magnetic centres open up, they interplay with each other, they exchange energy with each other and a certain synergy gets created.

A certain apparatus get created inside and in that apparatus the magnetic centre opens up, and then, when you listen to your guru, you get the deepest meaning from his words. You get deepest meaning because your capacity to digest it is so strong.

8

STRENGTH IN FLEXIBILITY & FLEXIBILITY IN STRENGTH

atvevaham jatu nasam na tvam neme janadhipah
Na chaiva na bhavisyamah sarve vayamatah param.

It is not as though neither you, nor I, nor these kings have never existed before; nor is it that we shall cease to exist in the future.

Look deeply into the above verse. When the magnetic centres open up in you through yoga, they open up your sensory acumen which becomes so sharp that you will not see merely the meaning of the master's words, but the essence of what he is trying to say.

For a word is an indicator indicating the indicated which is other than the indicator.

A word is only a pointer pointing out the pointed which is other than the pointer. And if you look at Lord Krishna's life also, there, as also in his teachings, you find a great sutra – there is flexibility in his strength and there is strength in his flexibility.

The teaching of Lord Krishna is in the Bhagavad Gita and in the Bheeshma Parva of the Mahabharata. The Bhagavatam looks at Lord Krishna's life itself, from which you can pick up a very important maxim, which is reflected in his teaching. It is important for your own personal excellence. In his life, there is flexibility in strength, and there is strength in flexibility.

I talked about how you have to create a harmony in conflict. You also have to know how to harmonise your internal energy. When I say that in Lord Krishna's life and teachings, there is flexibility in strength and strength in flexibility, it is about harmonizing internal energy, the combination of male and female energy.

Lord Krishna's life was tremendously flexible, and with intelligence. Flexibility without intelligence is a weakness. He helped Arjuna in eloping with his own sister, that's tremendous flexibility. But there is also strength in Lord Krishna which is a male energy, and there is a flexibility which is a female energy, and the two mix and interplay with each other. It is like how the harmonium, the flute and the tabla interplaying with each other in a certain rhythm, in a certain harmony, create beautiful music.

It is an important maxim in warfare, and in the Indian literature – you should be flexible and at the same time you should be strong. Therefore Indian gurus invariably are on the banks of a river.

The river is one of the important symbols of Hinduism. The strength of the river is in its commitment to go towards the ocean. The river does not know it is going to the ocean, but there is intuitively a certain commitment which can be called strength – it is committed to go towards the ocean, no matter what obstacles it faces.

From the Himalayas the river Ganges goes all the way to the Bay of Bengal, regardless of obstacles. If it encounters an obstacle like a rock, the river is so flexible, it goes round the obstacle and still keeps going. The river has the strength to go towards the ocean, and also the flexibility to go towards it. So when you are seated next to the river, this is the message you have to learn intuitively. When your sensory sharpness increases you learn this, you just go on looking at the river, and the river Ganges is very meditative, has very positive energy, so you bow down, and the river starts conveying to you that in life also you need flexibility, and you need strength.

This principle is used in the art of war. Your enemy is there, you should be flexible, and the flexibility should enhance your strength and your strength should enhance your flexibility. I am going leave it little vague, not because I am vague about it, but because some of us think, many of us think we think and most of us never think of thinking.

So if I keep it little vague, I want your receptor to see what can be the meaning and sometimes you may get a meaning which is more than what I have understood. That is the art of teaching. Sometimes it is only when someone talks above the head that you realise you have a head.

In the Gita when Lord Krishna says, "Vyvasayatmika buddhihi rekhehe kurunandana," it is nothing but strength, the strength of a commitment that I am going to reach my goal. The river does not know it will reach the goal, but it is committed to move forward, and the river reaches the goal of the ocean, even though, at the source in the Himalayas, it does not know that it is going towards the ocean.

The very power of commitment which guides you is

divine. So we should have the commitment to reach the goal. But rigid strength will not help. You should also be flexible like a river. Whatever obstacle comes our way, we should go through. So flexibility is in strength and strength lies in flexibility.

In martial art we say you should be like a bamboo, not like a tree. A tree, when a heavy breeze comes, will fall down. But the bamboo will bend, it is flexible, at the same time strong. It can come back. So therefore there is strength in the flexibility, flexibility in the strength. In warfare it is an important principle that you should be like a bamboo, flexible, and when it hits back, it hits with tremendous force.

On the other hand, the tree is strong, but not flexible. It just falls. In life also you need flexibility. If you want your marriage to be successful you should be flexible. At the same time you should be strong in your commitment also.

By winning you lose, by losing you win. You know how beautiful the power of martial art is, when somebody comes and touches you, you hit him. That fellow falls. So you have won, but this fellow comes back with 200 other people to beat you up. What happens then is that by winning you lose.

But if somebody hits you, you know you can hit him back and break his head, but you also know that if he touches you, you will lose only for the time being. By losing you win your peace of mind. So by winning you lose, by losing you win.

Therefore, in the art of war, it is very important that you should have flexibility in strength and strength in flexibility.

You have flexibility when you know how to deeply accept a fact. "Agathe swagatham kuriyat gacchantham na nivarayet." "Agathe swagatham," once you have the power of acceptance which is a female energy, then you can be flexible. People who are rigid cannot accept. Arjuna is not able to accept the fact that he has to fight Bhishma and Drona, his grandsire and his own master. He is committed, that is male energy, but what is missing, is the acceptance of the fact that life is sometimes like this. He is not able to accept that reality.

The fact of life is that you have to learn to accept realities. Even when you get confused just accept it. That is called flexibility. But acceptance without strength is looseness. Only strength without acceptance is too rigid, like a tree. You have to learn to have strength and also accept.

9

COMMUNICATION – FROM ONE PRESENCE TO ANOTHER PRESENCE

o in the Gita the Lord talks about acceptance and learning to accept, which is the female energy. He talks about how one should be committed and not scattered, and this is a part of male energy. And when you have both male and female energies, when you have strength and flexibility, and they interplay with each other, the result is what is called a "surabhi."

Then the magnetic centre opens up, then there is the intellectual acumen, there is an emotional acumen, there is the body acumen and in that acumen, you will see the essence of what the master says, and not just the words.

The communication between Lord Krishna and Arjuna is not strictly verbal. It is from one presence to another presence. When the conches are blown, and all are ready to fight, then suddenly Arjuna asks Lord Krishna to place his chariot between both the armies.

Then Krishna takes the chariot to the middle, Arjuna gets up, looks at the Pandavas, looks at the Kauravas and the breakdown happens. When the breakdown happens, Lord Krishna gives the teachings. While he gave him the divine teachings, all of 17 chapters, do you imagine the Kauravas were patiently waiting, after the conches had been blown and the Pandavas also were waiting?

The communication would have happened in an esoteric way. Adi Shankaracharya, in the Dakshinamurthy Ashtakam says, "Mouna vakya prakatita para brahma thatvam yuvanam," which means that between the guru and shishya, communication happens through "*mouna,*" through silence, from one presence to another presence. Between Krishna and Arjuna, it is communication from one presence to another presence.

Gross persons can never understand this, because the gross person understands only the body of religion. A little subtler person understands the mind of religion and the deepest person can understand the soul of religion. The body of religion consists of only rituals. Not that it is bad, but that is the outer layer of religion. Go a little more into religion, like breaking the coconut, which means you are breaking your ego, your "*ahamkara,*" and you get the mind of religion. Then see the soul of religion, which is nothing but purity and silence.

Therefore, there is the body of religion, the mind of religion, the soul of religion. When you come to the soul of religion, even in this communication between you and me, if you get just my words it is only the body of the lecture, if you get my meaning, it is only the mind of the lecture, and if your presence and my presence can mix with each other, like strength mixes in flexibility, then by presence-to-presence interaction a "*sphota,*" an outburst of energy happens. Real communication between guru and shishya is presence to presence.

That is how a simple butterfly became a guru of Dattatreya, a river became a guru of Dattatreya, a bee and an ant became gurus of Dattatreya. A flower taught so much to Dattatreya, but so many people look at the flower and nothing happens. Space (*Akasha*), Air (*vayuhu*), Fire (*Agnihi*), water (*Apaha*), Earth (*Prithvi*), Sun (*Surya*), butterfly (*Titilaha*), Moon (*Chandraha*) – they all became gurus to Dattatreya.

The presence has to open up, and for that the magnetic centre has to open up. Your focus should be there. If that is not the focus, what you get is only superficial. By the blessing of the Lord feel the magnetic emotional and intellectual centres open up, feel the magnetic body centre open up and feel all the three centres interplay with each other like how in the body your eyes, nose and your heart interplay with each other. So feel the three centres mysteriously interplay with the blessings of the Lord, and feel yourself blessed. So truth is unfolded in "*mouna*," silence, and therefore the real communication is from one presence to another presence.

10

FROM PRISON TO PRESENCE

ou must understand that our body can become a prison and, that we have to transform the body into a presence. Your emotions can become a prison, but they should become a presence. So too, your intellect can be a prison. This happens by wrong thinking, by conditioned thinking, but this prison has to become a certain presence.

Therefore, from a prison to presence, should be the overall vision. "Asatoma sadgamya, tamasoma jyotir gamaya, mrityorma amrutam gamaya." This well known chant means, lead me from the unreal to real, from darkness to light, from death to immortality.

Throughout the Bhagavad Gita the Lord through his teachings, is basically liberating us from shackles (Samsara) and leading us to freedom (Nirvana). If it is not treated properly, if it is abused improperly and if there is a high sense of indiscipline, this wonderful body can become a burden; but it can also become a spring board for wonderful action.

Therefore in the Gita the Lord says, "Yukta ahara viharasya yukta shrestrasya karmasu;" everywhere, "*yukta*," be moderate in your "*ahara*," food, be moderate in your "*vihara*," in your activity, be moderate in your entertainment. Learn the moderateness that the Lord Buddha speaks of in his theory – the middle path, "majjam nikaya."

The Buddha's whole teaching is called "majjam nikaya," the golden middle path and if you read the Gita, you find the Lord, much before, has talked about being moderate there. So, if you discipline the body, it is not going to be a burden, it is going to become, instead of a prison, a presence. That discipline, the discipline of Hatha yoga, is also mentioned in Gita.

For bringing enhancement in personal excellence, we have emotion. Emotion means energy in motion. And if these emotions are not disciplined, harmonised, and harnessed through Bhakti yoga, the yoga of devotion, then you find these emotions can become a prison.

If you look at somebody who is happy, you become unhappy thinking, "How come that rascal is happy when I am unhappy?" You see somebody wearing diamond earrings, and think, "My husband has given me only golden earrings," so you become angry with the husband by looking at someone's diamond earrings.

If the emotions are not properly trained through the discipline of Bhakti yoga, the yoga of devotion, they can go haywire. The emotions have to be purified.

In the Bhagavad Gita the Lord says, devotion is not about doing a great *havan* – a fire ritual – even though performing *havan* is a beautiful discipline. You can offer a flower, you can offer water, or a leaf, what you offer is not important, the devotion with which you offer is more important. "Patram, pushpam, palam, toyam, yo bhaktiya prayachati."

So with this devotion, this *"bhavana,"* this Bhakti, if you can convert whatever activities you do, *"sarvani karmani,"* into an offering unto the Lord, then your emotions which are indisciplined, or which are erratic, which can create prisons for you, those emotions then become a presence.

Therefore, in my LIFE workshop, when I say, can you do what you love and also love what you do, I'm just giving the translation, because in the Gita you find all these. Can you really do what you really love? Most of us do not have the courage to do what we love. If you do what you love, you may be a painter.

The Lord says in the Gita, better a death following your *"swadharma"* than in following something else. Even if death comes in fulfilling what is *"swadharma,"* doing what you really love, better to die in doing that. If you have the courage to do what you love, then there is a tremendous fulfillment in such an act, so the first thing is to do what you love. In my LIFE workshop I always say that you must have the *"veerarasa,"* the courage to do what you love.

I come from a business family. My whole family is in business. But I love this path of spirituality; I love the path of preaching, so I do it even though it is uncertain what the future is for me. But when you do what you love to do, there is a fulfillment in the process. To do this, you need one of the *"navarasas,"* you need the *"veerarasa."* You need courage to do that.

In the Kathopanishad it is said that it is the courageous person who can really see himself.

"Kaschit dheeraha pratyagatmaanam aikshatu."

So you have to do what you really love.

Then you have to learn to love what you do. And if you learn to love what you are doing, and do what you love, a certain discipline will silently happen in your emotional centre, and from a mechanical emotional center, it becomes a magnetic emotional center. So, through the discipline of Bhakti yoga there is certain personal excellence achieved.

You may ask, for one who works in the corporate world, how is this relevant? More than what you say, how you feel when you give expression is important.

Therefore, in management, they say you should build up your emotional bank account. If you are giving right instructions without really feeling and caring for a person, if you don't build up an emotional bank account among your people in the corporate world, you never create a sense of belongingness or sense of feeling connected.

And therefore, even in the corporate world you should feel what you say. And your feeling should be one of caring. Feeling should really connect people, and that is what the magnetic emotion centre does. If your emotions are not trained, not disciplined, they will become prisons to you by your jealousy, anger, and frustration, when instead they should become a wonderful presence.

Your intellectual centre can also become a prison. But, through Gnana yoga, that prison can be transformed and become a presence. The Lord in the Gita says, "Nahi gnanena sadrisham pavithram iha vidyathe" – there is nothing purer than knowledge. By the discipline of yoga of understanding (*gnana yoga*), your mind, your "*buddhi*," which can become a prison, becomes a presence.

When Swami Vivekananda, in the Parliament of World Religions in Chicago said, "Brothers and sisters of America," the words were very few, only five words, but before he even completed his speech, he had a standing ovation. It was not the words, it was the presence of Swami Vivekananda which touched people.

When we say Mahatma Gandhi touched people, it was the presence. And therefore this presence is very important.

The quintessence of the Gita is to move from a prison to a presence, or, in other words, to turn a mechanical centre into a magnetic centre. From mechanical emotion you have to make it magnetic emotion; your intellect which is in mechanical thinking should be made magnetic. If you don't do so, your thinking can also bind you.

Like I mentioned earlier, there is the body of religion, there is the mind of religion, and there is the soul of religion. And if you are not into the soul of religion, then religion can also bind you. Most of the people who are in conflict in religion are looking only at the body of religion, which is the periphery – the rituals, the tradition, the way in which you dress the body.

The mind of religion is about understanding, for example, why one wears a saffron dress. You understand in your mind why you are doing this. Saffron represents fire; just as fire dispels darkness, the fire of knowledge has to dispel ignorance, so the very colour itself has that impact.

Therefore, the need for sleep is less for those who wear a fire colour dress. You put your *chandan* – sandal paste – on the forehead because the intuitive centre has to open up. So this is the mind of religion. The soul of religion is silence, it is "*shuddha*," purity, it is innocence, "*asmita*." So if you don't know this, religion itself can be binding. That is why in the name of religion there is so much of bloodshed. Religion is not responsible for this, but your mechanical understanding is.

Even though I am a Swamiji I am a lover of sports. For me sports is a beautiful discipline. Until recently I was playing basketball. I was the captain of a basketball team when I was young. So I continued playing the game as a part of discipline.

One of my students saw me playing basketball, and became utterly confused. He said, "Swamiji, I am extremely disturbed." I said, "Why, what happened?" "Because you are playing basketball. A Swamiji should not play basketball," he said. I said, "Who has to decide that? Certainly not you... as you have not given me the ball." He said, "In Lord Krishna's time Swamijis were not playing basketball."

People are so logical.

That is why in *tarka sastra* – the book of logic – it is said that if a stupid person learns logic, the logic becomes stupid. And I said, "In Lord Krishna's time there was no basketball." Lord Krishna, in his life, was so playful, so innocent, so unconditioned; and the so-called devotees of Lord Krishna are highly serious.

The contradiction is because intellect, instead of understanding the soul of Lord Krishna's teachings, gets only the body of it. It is stuck at the periphery of the teaching and misses the very soul. That is how your intellect also can be binding. If the prison does not become presence, you will miss the poetry and the beauty of life.

There is a story about Mulla Nazruddin, the Sufi. His wife gives him one gold coin and says, "Please get three donkeys. And be careful, three donkeys, not more not less." His wife was really a female wrestler, in terms of her looks, and her presence. Mulla was a philosopher, so he went and got three donkeys and sat on one of them and on his way back, he got lost in his soliloquy.

Suddenly, when he was near home he remembered what his wife said, "Get three donkeys." And he now counted, one .... two... and the third is missing. And he was extremely scared. Generally men are scared of their wives. They may say they are the boss, but definitely they are scared. He checked his pocket – no gold coin. Then he decided, "Let me be honest."

Sometimes people practice honesty when there is no other way out. So he went to the house, his wife was standing there, and he said, "I know you gave me one gold coin, I know you told me to get three donkeys, I do not know how but there are only two donkeys." And for first time the Mulla's wife smiled, and said, "I don't see two donkeys, I see four donkeys." Mulla was seated on the third donkey.

Lord Krishna in the Gita says, "Navadwarepuredehi," in the nine-gated city called the body, "sukham aasthe," we are seated in joy, but what are we doing? We are lost outside. Unless we take a dip within ourselves, our whole life is going to be lost, but you can look within yourself provided your mind allows you to do so.

Our mind does not allow us to look within ourselves. Why? Because our mind is programmed to look out. The Katha Upanishad says, "Paraanchikani yatrunatu swayambhuhu" – we are always looking out. Hence Saint Kabir says, our mind is like a grinding machine, "Chalti chakki dekhike diya kabira roi." Therefore anything which is put in it is not saved – "sabath bachana koi." Nothing is saved. And he says, "Ghat ander anahat garjai isme uthat pukar" – in the pot called the body, silence is roaring, joy is roaring, but you cannot look because your mind is like the grinding machine, mechanical, so it is always looking out.

Hence for personal excellence you have to train the mind. The quintessence is that you can convert a prison into a presence through Karma yoga, through Hatha yoga, through Bhakti yoga, and through Gnana yoga. Then you find that personal excellence starts happening in your life. If you don't do that, life is going to be extremely miserable.

11

CREATE A HARMONY IN CHANGE: NOT A CONFLICT IN CHANGE

ust male energy is not enough in life; female energy is also needed, you should be flexible like a woman. To be flexible means you should have the power to accept. Lots of people do not have the power to accept.

When people say, "Swamiji, there is so much of unfairness in this world," I say, "Such is the way of life. Life is a combination of fair and unfair." So, if you don't have the power to accept, then you will find that every grey hair gives you depression. Some people come to me asking if there is a mantra for the hair to become black. I say that my own hair is greying. They do not have even the sense to see that. People's greed is so much, so they are not able to accept certain things.

They are not able to accept because of a certain rigidity, which is a prison habit of the *jeevatma* – the lower self. When you read the Gita you realize that you have to discover your prison habits and see how they erode and destroy your personal excellence.

Being rigid is a psychological prison habit. One of the rigidities people have is that they cannot stand insecurity.

You cannot accept a thing called insecurity, but the fact of life is that life is insecure.

But people are preprogrammed like the shows on TV. Except for one or two live programmes, most of TV programmes are preprogrammed. Similarly, when you look at people, when you look at life, when you look at certain things, you have preprogrammed opinions.

Somebody has an opinion about the Gita that it is not applicable in our lives. A managing director of a company who met me in the airport told me, "I have listened to one talk of yours, Swamiji, on the TV; I heard you are a management guru, but I don't think Gita is applicable in that context." I said, "Have you read the Gita?" He said, "No." So he has not read the Gita but he has an opinion on it.

This is called being psychologically preprogrammed. When you are preprogrammed what happens? You look at life with the preprogrammed mind. So, if you are looking in this way, you are not really looking. You are seeing only a programming.

Therefore, in Zen it is said, not seeing, is seeing. Why do they say that? Because very often, our seeing is... in fact, not seeing. How come our seeing is not seeing? Because when we look at someone, immediately the preprogrammed mind labels that person. And the moment you label somebody you don't see the person, you see the label. Then you develop a liking towards the person, or you dislike the person.

But are you developing a liking or disliking towards the person or towards the label? We are only relating to the label. And we call this seeing. So Zen says, "not seeing is seeing."

So, with this type of mind you look at life, and... you say, I don't like insecurity. In fact, insecurity is not what you don't like, what you label as insecurity is what you don't like. And then you develop a philosophy that insecurity is not comfortable, and security is solace, and you become rigid. You create a philosophy, then you start justifying the philosophy, then you become imprisoned in that philosophy.

But instead of that, just drop those labels. That is why philosophy in Sanskrit is called "Darshan Sastra," because "darshan" means seeing. Drop all the labels and just look at insecurity. How can insecurity be uncomfortable? Insecurity is nothing but change. When you say, "I am insecure," it means that something is changing. Something is not consistent. And your mind is preprogrammed to want something to be consistent. And the fact of life is that life is inconsistent.

One of my student, was shot and he started bleeding. In the case of another student who was in the bathroom, whose wife was saying coffee is ready, had a heart attack and died. Life is not consistent. Everything is "kshanikam," or momentary. That is life. It is very unfair, but that is life. You have a philosophy that it should be fair. And then you justify the philosophy. That is the problem.

Anything can happen at any time. In other words, it is nothing but change. If you look at change without a label, with a sense of openness, then you find that every change is God's mechanism of throwing a surprise.

So each moment is a surprise. And therefore, you are participating in the miracle of the moment, the magic of the moment and each moment is a surprise and you are participating in the miracle of life. What that moment is, you don't know. You are available to participate, like a swimmer swims with the waves. If you do this, change becomes God's gift for you to participate in. But then what happens? You look at change, and immediately you label it with your insecurity label, so insecurity is bad and change is bad.

That is why in management, change management is a buzzword. And therefore, the important philosophy in the Gita is, create a harmony in change. Just as you create a harmony in conflict, create a harmony in change. Don't create a conflict in change.

In the 13th verse of chapter II, the Lord says that when you are born to youth, you are dead to childhood, when you die to youth you are born to middle age. When you are dead to middle age, you are born to old age; and when you die you are born to another body. So those who realize this remain calm in life.

I will not go into a word-by-word meaning. Let us draw the essence now, since we are discussing the topic of personal excellence through the Gita.

In quintessence, the verse says, create a harmony in change. Don't create a conflict in change, because life is constantly changing.

The Lord says, your body goes through youth, and grows old. In other words, the body is going through change, so create harmony in this change, not conflict. Some people resist change. They resist even the normal process of hair turning into grey.

That is why a lot of people lie about age. If they are 20, they say I am 22. If they are 30, they say 27, and when they reach 60 they say I am 65 to show that in spite of being old, I look young. They are so troubled by the natural phenomenon of the body going through a change. A grey hair comes and immediately they have to dye it.

Why are we creating a conflict? Grey hair is grey, black is black. A rose is rose, a lily is a lily. Deep within, there is a resistance to change. These are prison habits. And when you continue with the prison habits, you create worry and conflict. That is why the etymological meaning of the word "worry" is to twist and turn. We are unnecessarily creating conflict.

When the body is going through a change, just create a harmony in the change. Summer has its beauty, winter has its beauty and the rainy season has its beauty. In Bangalore, when there is summer, they do a rain dance. They create artificial rain in discos and dance. When it rains, they dance inside the room. We live so unnaturally with life, and then we suffer. Instead, go with the flow. The Lord says in the verse, create a harmony in change.

So, the first time someone calls you uncle, don't feel confused and say, "Don't call me uncle." You resist change because your present prison habits say that change is not ok. That is something preprogrammed. And when you have the preprogrammed habit excellence is not going to flow. Your intelligence flows when you are in harmony with what is.

So the Lord says that the wise person is not going to be disturbed because he has this understanding that they are events in life, they are internal states in life. Let me put it like this. When you are born, it is an event, when you get married, it is an event, and life is nothing but chain of events. With our prison habits we think events decide the course of our lives. That is a big illusion according to the Gita. Events do not decide the condition of your life; it is your inner state which decides it.

I go to Zurich every year since I have a centre there. Zurich is the most beautiful place in the world. Winters are magical and summers are magical. It is the only city in the world where every apartment should have a nuclear basement. If you have four flats you should have four nuclear basements. Life is not as hectic as in San Francisco. Everything is beautiful. But every time I take a workshop there, somebody says, "I am in depression, Swamiji, please help me."

Therefore, in the workshop I created a jargon – all of you are kings and queens. I started it there, but now I am using this everywhere.

All of you are kings and queens. What does this mean? It means that what a king and queen did not have 100 years back, you have now. A king and queen did not have a mobile, but you and I have; a king and queen did not have a computer, but you and I have; a king and queen did not have a washing machine, but you and I have.

So what a king and queen did not have, you and I have. Then why don't we experience ourselves to be like the King and the Queen? Because, the neighbour also has a mobile.

Everybody has got it, so what is so great about it. You see, in your mind, there is a prison habit, a deleting mechanism which comes and deletes the richness of who you are. Let us say your computer has beautiful programming in it; there is a virus which comes and de-programmes this wonderful computer, and therefore you have to install anti-virus software. So too, God has given us a wonderful mechanism, a wonderful software, by which, if each one of us evaluates ourselves, we are multimillionaires.

One of the leading dailies had brought out an article once which said that if each one of you sells your kidney, your liver, your marrow, your heart, your eyes, your nose, everything, you will be multimillionaires. Being multimillionaires, we don't care ... what is the big deal. We go on comparing and whipping ourselves. Therefore, we cannot experience the richness of who we are.

You have to feel this. Thinking is one level of understanding, feeling is another level of understanding and being is yet another level of understanding. So don't stop at thinking, otherwise you will have obesity in the head. It has to get into the feeling, don't even stop at feeling and get into being.

Therefore, Lord Krishna addresses the thinking, the feeling and the "being." In fact, thinking to feeling to being is the whole track of the Gita. So there is so much of richness in you; but you unnecessarily start comparing and become miserable.

These are prison habits. So when there is change, create a harmony in the change. How do you do that? You can create a harmony if you are at peace with what is and not resistant to what is, and then you can be at peace even if every hair falls off. When things are falling, unnecessarily we resist it, but the moment we resist it we are not in harmony with it. This is the knack you have to learn. A knack cannot be taught – it has to be caught. That is why a teaching cannot be taught; even though we teach, it has to be caught.

My mother was asking me one day, we are old people now, our legs are paining, and we are uncomfortable, how can we meditate? But I've noticed that my mother is very good at floating.

At the age of 60, she started learning floating, and the coach who taught her was himself surprised and said, "You are floating better than me." How did she learn that? Because it is a knack, and the moment she caught the knack she became better than her coach. I told her that meditation is also a knack. A knack cannot be taught – it has to be caught.

What is life? People think living for 60 years or 70 years is one's life span. But don't define life at such a macro level. Say one year is life. Is one year a life? No, it is not one year, it is one month. Not even one month is life – it is one day; don't take it as one day, say one hour; don't take it as one hour, take it as one minute; don't take it as one minute, it is this moment.

Right now, forget that you are going to live for 70 years. The lethargy comes because we think that we are going to live for 70 years. So everything can be done tomorrow. Like how every New Year, you make resolutions, and next year you do it afresh. Don't look at life like this. Don't treat your life as if it is 70 years long, because the moment you think that way, certain lethargy sets in. But life is not 70 years. Life is not one year, life is not one month, or one hour, or one minute. It is this moment. In the very next moment, life can disappear. Since life is this moment, live this moment in harmony. How do you float while swimming? You just do that; suddenly, you get the knack.

So just get the knack and live this moment. Practice living this moment. And in this moment be total and be fully at peace with it. In floating, if you put tension into it, you cannot float. You have to put in an effortless effort, which is a knack. The knack grows in you.

So forget that your life is 70 years long and live right now, this moment. And in this moment be total. Be at peace. Be at harmony with this moment. Once you get this, you will have discovered a master key. The master key is that you can be at this moment alive to the flow. At any time, just think of that moment, just be in harmony with life, and you will see that moment as a tremendous aliveness. The moment is not alive because your mind comes in and says, "I am 70 years old, 10 years back life was much better, 20 years back life was much more better, etc." You start comparing.

You are 70 years old, and 20 years ago you were jumping around and now you see others jumping around, and you say, "How cruel God has been to me." Instead of that, just forget it. If you are limping see the beauty of limping. Limping is like a break dance, there is certain rhythm in which you can limp and walk. If you come to my workshop I will demonstrate that.

A kind of limping in a graceful form, in a break dance, is called duck walk. So this duck walk, your body wave, your hand wave, everything can become like a dance. Then you see that the moment is wonderful. Old age is tremendously beautiful. Youth is tremendously beautiful. Middle age is beautiful. If you are ignorant that is also so beautiful. If you are unenlightened that also is so beautiful, because enlightened people cannot be as free as unenlightened people.

You cannot expect the Buddha to come and watch a movie like "Rangeela." But any "buddhu" can watch "Rangeela" with a cup of tea on his head. An unwise person has the freedom of doing whatever he can do, whereas the wise man is constricted to do only certain things.

See the beauty of being unenlightened. Only then you become enlightened. When you accept your un-enlightenment as the expression of the divine, then you will be enlightened. You have to learn to gracefully accept un-enlightenment as also God's gift. Just experience the ignorance. Sometimes ignorance is so beautiful.

Someone who was one of my classmates in college came and met me, and did my workshop. After the workshop, he said, "I feel depressed." I got confused. Generally, after my workshop people go home dancing. He says he feels depressed.

Why? He says, "Swamiji, you are such a wonderful speaker. We both played marbles together, and now you have become a wonderful speaker, but look at my life, how miserable it is." This fellow has come in a beautiful car and his wife looks like a film actress.

So what is his problem? "It is the same wife, I've seen somebody's sister and she is much better." Your mind cannot see the beauty of what is. That is the whole problem.

My classmate was unnecessarily comparing himself with me. If a tiger compares itself with a butterfly, it can get very miserable. And similarly, the butterfly comparing itself with anything else will be miserable. There is no end.

God has made each one a miracle. To live is to validate the miracle of the moment. The problem is we are not in the moment and therefore we are not in harmony with the moment, because we have the rigid prison habit of worrying, and of fear.

People have unnecessary fears. Even if you have fear, be at peace with it, harmonise with fear. In my workshop I make some people come up and talk. And their legs will be shaking, and hands will be trembling. I say, "Be at peace with your legs shaking." People go to the disco to make it shake. They pay money and go to the disco and shake beautifully.

Therefore I say, "Stop your preprogrammed feeling that this is fear. Just experience the shaking. Say it is beautiful. It is wonderful that your legs are shaking. Sing that old English song – "shake it to the right, shake it to the left, do the hippy hippy shake." By this process, I make them get into harmony with what is. Even fear has a beauty. But if you are not able to see such beauty, then you are not in harmony with what is, then you create a conflict with what is and that conflict creates chaos.

The president of a certain country won the election and went to the barber's shop, because the next day, he was supposed to give an address. He said, "Give me a good haircut." Recently, he had gone through divorce also. The barber started cutting his hair.

As he cut, he said, "You know, you have become the President, but do you know what your divorced wife said?"

"What did she say?" he asked.

The barber said, "She said you won the election because you look like a cross breed between a donkey and a buffalo."

His anger came up. And again the barber said, "You know what else your divorced wife said? She said you won not because of your intelligence, but because the people were stupid."

And yet again the barber said as he cut his hair, "You know what your divorced wife said?"

Now the President got very angry and said, "I have come for a haircut and not to know what my wife said."

The barber said, "It is helping me very much sir, because every time I say, you know what your wife said, your hair stands erect, and it is easy for me to cut."

People's habits have become like this. You pose, you present a mask. The moment you pose, you carpet your real feeling, which is pushed into the subconscious. When your real feeling is pushed into subconscious, then your subconscious becomes hurt, you don't heal the hurt and what you do is you spin the past hurt into an imaginative future. It is very simple. Sometimes, even though you are unhappy, you pose as if you are happy. That is also a discipline.

But be careful in this discipline. What happens in the posturing is that you keep pushing the real feeling into the subconscious. Then the past hurt is not healed. In order to heal, a hurt needs wisdom. So what happens when you project the hurt into the future is your whole life becomes a psychodrama of stupidity. And therefore we must not cheat ourselves in the way we pose.

A plane develops a problem in mid-air, over the sea, and everybody gets panicky. The airhostess says, "Do not worry, we have a beautiful device by which we can land on the sea. All those who know swimming come to the left side of the plane. All those who do not know swimming come to the right side of the plane."

Accordingly, they all came to either side. And then she said, "All those who know swimming, please jump out of the plane, it is only 20 km to the shore, and all those who do not know swimming thank you for flying with us."

What is the "thank you" for?

Some people's courtesy has no depth at all. Some people's smiles have no depth at all.

We develop pseudo smiles. We develop frustration habits. And when you develop these frustration habits, these lying habits, worrying habits and fear habits, and if you don't change them, they will make you resist seeing the beauty of what is.

And therefore, if we can cleanse ourselves of that prison habit, the preprogramming habit that says that I define what the moment should be – when you stop thinking like that, you can be in harmony with what is. If you are not in harmony with what is, it will lead to a conflict with what is. Then you never see the beauty of what is because your mind is caught up in the dogma of how beauty should be. With this as the background, look at the verse* where the Lord says that when you are born to youth, you are dead to childhood, when you die to youth you are born to middle age. When you are dead to middle age, you are born to old age; therefore, death is constantly happening, death does not happen only at the end of life, it happens every moment.

Therefore, "Gatasunagatasumshca nanushochanti panditah," the wise person does not grieve for the dead, nor for the living. Death is not alien to life, death is happening every moment. Change happens every moment, and death is also a form of change.

"Prathama malla nibaharana nyaya:" a Sanskrit saying which means that if you knock off the number one person, you've knocked off everybody else. If you want to be the heavy weight champion knock off the existing heavy weight champion. Then you are the heavy weight champion of the world and you don't have to knock off all those people whom the heavy weight champion has finished off. Similarly, the biggest fear people have is the fear of death. The Lord says that death is also a change. Change is not something alien, it is happening all the time. There is beauty in change and you should see it. Therefore, the courageous person is not going to die.

---

* Dehinosminyatha dehe kaumaram yauvanam jara.
  Tatha dehantarapraptirdhirastatra na muhyati.

Therefore, do not treat death as insecurity, it is not alien, it is a form of a change. Now look at the beauty of what is and not with the dogma of what should be. You are not in harmony with what is, you are in harmony with a dogma, a rigid framework of what should be, and you see that as beauty.

Death is also beauty. You have been fired from the job – that is also beauty. You will say, "You are not in a job, Swamiji, so you do not know." Very few of you can understand that I am rejoicing that I am not permanently in a job. "Shraddavan labhate gnanam," is a saying which means have the "*shraddha*" or faith that if one door closes, the other door opens. In personal excellence it is a very powerful belief system.

If this moment closes, another moment opens. If anything dies, something new has to be born. Don't be afraid of death. Death is also a wonderful experience. Death is also a form of change, it has a certain beauty. You are not able to see the beauty of death because you have an addiction towards life. You have a dogma of what security is, therefore you cannot see the beauty of insecurity. Drop the preprogramming.

Therefore, the Lord says that death is with you right from childhood, because when you are dead to childhood, you are born to youth, when dead to youth, born to middle age, when dead to middle age, born to old age, so death is constantly happening. Death is change.

Therefore there is in the Gita the deep belief that if one door closes, the other door opens. For your personal excellence, know that if this job goes another job will come, because life is about change. If your spouse leaves you it does not matter, if one idiot goes, another idiot will come. Take it lightly but not loosely. Don't be serious. Some people say so seriously, "Swamiji, I want to be enlightened." Then enlightenment becomes the personification of un-enlightenment.

12

THE CHANGELESS PRINCIPLE

he Lord says, the body goes through the changes of childhood, youth and old age ("kaumaram, yauvanam, jara"). But something inside the body is the same in childhood, and in middle age, and in old age. I am young, I am middle aged, I am old. The body has gone through death and change, but change can happen only if there is a changeless principle. And the changeless principle is something in you that is unpolluted.

Discover that changeless being. I am young, then I become middle aged. Middle age and youth change, but the "I" is the same – the "I" in youth is the same as the "I" in middle age and old age.

So instead of seeing the periphery of you, see the very core of you. If you want to bring excellence in any issue see the core of the issue. The Lord says when you look at yourself, don't see the periphery of yourself and see the core of yourself. You say things are changing; yet there is a contrast called a changeless principle.

Intelligent people should ever be grateful to fools, because if fools do not exist, intelligent people cannot be defined. If you say, "I am intelligent, Swamiji, and I am upset with my subordinate who is a fool," I say that your fool is a contrast from which you get defined as intelligent.

If everybody is intelligent then what is the essence of intelligence?

The intelligent is only a contrast with the unintelligent. So every intelligent person should be very grateful to the unintelligent person.

Everything exists in contrast. So the periphery of you is changing and the core of you is not changing. To work on your personal excellence, look at the core of you. If you know the knack of looking at the core of you, then, what happens is that when you look at a problem, you look at the core of the problem, and you will not look at the periphery of the problem.

The periphery has a beauty, the core has a beauty; therefore, in life, when you look at the problem, look at the core, and when you look at the core, you will not be upset with the periphery because the periphery exists only in the contrast to the core. So you don't get upset by the periphery of the problem.

Therefore the Lord says, things are changing, but something in you is not changing; O Arjuna, look at the core, there is an unpolluted centre in us. On the surface of the ocean there are waves, but deep inside the ocean there is certain stillness. The waves of the ocean are beautiful. In the depth of the ocean there is stillness. Discover the totality of the ocean. Discover the totality of you.

The periphery of you is change, death; there is also the core of you that is changeless. And if you don't discover the core of you, then, without knowing yourself you are living in the world. That is a maddening attitude towards life. Know yourself. In that core there is a pure centre, an unpolluted centre, in all of us. In the Patanjali Yoga Sutra it is called "asmita," and if you don't discover this "asmita," intelligence and excellence will never grow.

Having understood this with "Buddhi yoga," means the yoga of knowledge, use "Bhakti yoga" to pray to the Lord for the blessing of discovering the center, not living only in the periphery, and dip into your own self with love, with the blessings of the Lord.

13

THE ABSENCE OF PRESENCE AND THE PRESENCE OF ABSENCE

Another very important verse for developing personal excellence is the 5th verse of chapter VI.* This verse talks about how, to bring about continuous improvement in your life, you have to work on your inner state, and not get lost in the events of life.

Most of us draw our energy from the events of life. If you are drawing the energy from events of life, then they become the remote control of your life. Somebody else is controlling your life. That is a kind of hell, because 'I' get defined by others' definition of who I am.

Often, your experience of "I" depends upon others' perception of you. If others perceive me as an intelligent speaker, as a good speaker, my "I" gets defined by what others say about me. When I get defined by others, then who is controlling my life? Others are controlling my life because my "I" is the creation of what others have said.

My "I" is not an experience of my inner state. It is an experience of what others have told me, so I have been created by others. If I have been created by others, I have a

---

* Uddharedatmanatmanam natmanamavasadayet.
  Atmaivahyatmalo bandhuratmaiva ripuratmanah.

103

dependence on others. The reason why we are so caught up in looking good is that others have to endorse us, because the "I" is the product of what others say. That is how we live on the periphery.

Therefore, Lord Krishna goes on talking to Arjuna about discovering the core of your-self. The peripheral "I" depends upon what others say about me. So we get caught up in looking good. But the teaching of the Gita is that your "absence should become a presence, and your presence should become your absence."

Our presence refers to our ego; the psychodrama of "who I am" is our presence. "Ahankara vimudhatma kartha iti manyate" – Lord Krishna says, "ahankara vimudhatma" – the egoistic person is a great fool. Why? Our presence, our ego, is the periphery of ourselves. And this periphery is created by what others have said about us. Therefore, we are constantly lost in pleasing others; so we cannot be authentic to ourselves.

What the Gita is inviting us into is a state where you do not play the ego drama. The absence of the "I" which is one's ego should become your presence. Your absence should become the presence and the presence should become your absence. That is why the Buddha used the word, *Annatta* – no self.

If you go to the Hindu temple in the south, called Chidambaram, you find *arti* is done to empty space. *Ambara* means space, Chidambaram means empty space. So what does it mean? It means that in the empty space you become *shunya*, an absence.

In the Chidambaram temple, when you do the arti to

empty space, it means if your presence is absence, next to it is Nataraja, who is dancing there. Nataraja dancing in the Chidambaram temple means that if your presence is your absence, and the absence of your ego is your presence, ecstasy will dance in your being; a beautiful symbol.

In our lives we are suffering because ego is our presence, but the enlightened person lives in such a way that his presence is his absence. All our struggles to be better than the other, to be number one, because of· which, parents give so much of tension to children to get the first rank, is the play of the ego. If everybody in the class is going to be first, who is to be second? It is how the ego plays a game.

Can your presence be the absence of "I?" Can emptiness be your presence? You will then find that a different intelligence happens. You ask any good player – that is why sports is very good thing to be in, and in Kaliyuga a spiritual person should be in sports.

For example, as you are playing tennis, you should be in the Chidambaram state, you should be empty. If you hit a shot thinking, "My girl friend is watching me, others are watching me," if that becomes your presence, you will miss the ball.

When you hit the shot, no matter who is praising you, or appreciating you, you should cut yourself from there, just be empty looking at the ball as it comes and allow the stroke to be made. You may miss it, but if you miss it, then you will learn what it is about. While you are playing the game, if you are not empty and focused, if you are not an absence, but an ego presence, your performance cannot be really good. Say you are playing basketball; as you play, if you start worrying, "Will I win, will I win," the worry becomes the presence, but when you play basketball you should freeze your mind, you should be empty like Chidambaram, and then, through the emptiness you should navigate yourself.

So your absence should become your presence, and your presence should be your absence. Many of our tensions happen because of the "I" that is sitting in the heart of our life. The Lord says in the Gita therefore, "Uddharet atmanaatmanam;" O Arjuna, lift yourself by your self to a state where you are nobody. The whole drama of being somebody is what you have to eliminate.

In Bombay, if you are somebody, you have a good flat. You will say, "Swamiji, come to my flat, I have a beautiful flat in Mumbai. It is my flat." "Is it your flat?" "Yes Swamiji, it is in Colaba, very expensive." This person says, "It is my flat." I say, "The ground, the floor on which we are standing, is the top of the bottom fellow. And the roof which you say is yours, is the bottom of the top fellow. The side is the side of other fellow. Which is your flat?"

"This space," you may say. The mosquitoes also say it is their space. So what is yours, actually? We live in an illusion that it is ours. Nothing is ours, really speaking.

If people say, "Swamiji, you are a good speaker," I have not created this brain, I have not created the slokas, I have created nothing. I find myself "nimita matram bhava" – I am just an instrument through which something is flowing.

I was thanking someone for giving a donation for feeding the poor and he said, "Swamiji, don't thank me. I myself have received a donation and that donation is what

I am giving. Where is my donation?" It touched me. That is why the Muslims have the expression "Insha Allah." God willing, it will happen. Don't take anything as yours.

A beautiful lady came to my workshop, and said, "Swamiji, I have a lot of tension. Everybody says I am beautiful, everybody appreciates me, but my husband is only fond of eating, he only eats." I know the husband, he has given so much of freedom to her, but what is her problem? "My husband is not appreciating me." "But he loves you," I asked, "and love is shown in different ways." "But he cannot appreciate me and because of that I am in depression, Swamiji," she said.

Nowadays, it has become a status symbol to say I'm depressed. Like, 40 years ago if you drank you were considered to be a bad person. Nowadays if you don't drink it appears you do not have high status. Even to swamijis they offer drinks.

During one of my Europe tour, a group of my students said, "Swamiji, beer is only barley water. It is very good actually. Wine is only grape juice, nothing in this, Swamiji." So this lady, she is in depression, because her husband is not appreciating her.

I told her, how big is the earth in the cosmos? A small, tiny dot. How big is India on the earth? A smaller dot. How big is this city, an even smaller dot? How big is this hall we are in, a smaller dot? And in this one hall we are 200 people and in that 200, where are you? A further, smaller dot. We are practically nobody, I said, and it is as ridiculous as if a mosquito comes in front of you and says, "Nobody is appreciating me".

But we live life as though we are in the centre of the cosmos, as though everybody has to worship us. We are living in this illusion, and this illusion is creating a delusion and in this delusion, we are suffering in life.

"Agnanena avritam gnanam tena muhyanti jantavaha." The Lord in the Gita says, "It is because of ignorance that man is deluded." Hence, the Lord says "Uddharet," lift yourself by your self, O Arjuna, to a state where absence becomes a presence. A river in the Himalays does not know it is going to go towards the ocean where it gets dissolved, but it simply flows naturally. A meditator does not know it is in the dissolution of the "I" that there is the real discovery of God.

In a state of deep sleep when your being is absence, look at it, what a beautiful state it is. Adi Shankaracharya says, "I did not know anything, but I slept extremely well."* You are in that state when you listen to music or look at the beautiful sunrise. When you are looking at something and you are no more there, then you experience a tremendous awe.

It is your absence which gives you a real presence. It is the presence of the ego which takes away the beauty of the absence. So let your presence be absence and your absence be a presence.

This state is this goal. "Uddharet atmanaatmanam," the Lord says. O Arjuna, lift yourself to the state of absence. He has to say lift yourself because ego exists, but "natmanam avasadayet" – don't condemn yourself. Don't get upset about why it is not happening. Every time you

---

* "Aham kimampi na jahnaami sukhena nidramaya anubhuyate."

fail, learn from your failure, every time you succeed, be grateful for such experience.

If you learn from your failure and you are grateful to your success, then "atma eva atmanaha banduhu," your mind becomes a friend, a "bandhu." The mind is no more going to be a prison, it is going to become a presence. And the presence is the very absence of the "I," or else your mind will be the "ripuhu," an enemy. You want to convert your mind into a friend.

The greatest task in personal excellence is that your mind should become a friend, it should not be an enemy. A friend is one who supports you. The enemy is one who counters you. When your mind supports you it brings joy. The way we use the mind by comparing unnecessarily, we get whipped, and we suffer from that.

14

EXTERNAL AND INTERNAL WORLDS

here is an external world; you are seeing me and I am seeing you that are one level of reality. There is an internal world, which is another level of reality.

Now, the important point is that your external world exists internally – as an impression, as a "vasana." I look at a table, the table exists in me as only an impression, as a "vasana."

More importantly, the external world, that is, your husband, your wife, your children, has one reality, "*vyvahara satya*" – empirical reality, but it exists in you as an impression, a "vasana." Now, what is more real to you? Is it the impression or the other reality? It is the impression. What is more real to you is not the external person – the external person exists in you as an impression. So, what is more real is the impression, not the external world.

So, Lord Krishna says, convert what is more real, i.e., impression, into a friend and achieve personal excellence. Further, the impression itself is also not the problem; the problem is the psychological climate in which the impression exists.

If I meet a person with the dress of a different religion,

and I look at him, he falls as an impression on my mind; then what happens to the impression is, "Hey, this man is a spy who has come here. I think he has come here to put a bomb." The impression exists in an internal climate which is interpreting and labeling.

So the impression is not a problem; the problem is that there is an interpretation in terms of a climate of anger, jealousy, hatred, etc., which is called *"aparaprakritihi,"* the lower nature, and in that climate the impression exists.

So, what happens is, the impression gets polluted by your internal climate, and then, with the polluted impression you look at the other person. The other person is then the extension of your inner pollution.

Therefore, the external world is one thing, but it falls as an impression in you, and you have to be aware that the outer experience is not just outer, it is also the inner impression. The impression does not always create a problem, just as religion itself does not create a problem.

But the impression exists in an internal state that has anger, jealousy, hatred, etc., which is the inner pollution and that decides how you experience that external event of other persons. The task is to free yourself from the inner pollution, the climate in which the impression exists.

If you free yourself from that, somebody can call you an idiot and that word, idiot, does not become an impression. In my LIFE workshop I say that if somebody calls you an idiot, doubly check yourself.

If your boss calls you an idiot, see that the word "idiot" is not the problem. It is a beautiful, juicy, aesthetic word.

Also, an idiot has such freedom to do whatever he wants. It is such a wonderful word, "idiot."

Someone said, "I am a Ph.D, Swamiji." I said that Ph.D means Permanent Head Damage. So if you are a Ph.D it is nothing to be upset about, and if you are an idiot, that also is nothing to be upset about. Because if you are an idiot, it is a statement of fact. If you are not an idiot, then there is nothing to be upset about.

So what is upsetting is not the word, it is not the impression, but the polluting factor in which it exists. There is a justifying mechanism, there is a lying mechanism, an ego mechanism, an anger mechanism, so there is always some consideration going on inside you. It is this climate that is the inner state. Unless you remove this negative inner state, it is not going to be possible for you to see that a rose is a rose, is a rose, is a rose.

There is a distinction between the events and inner states. The experience of life is not the events; the experience of life is your inner state.

One of my students from Hyderabad flew down to Mumbai to make his relative to do my workshop. Five or six years ago, that relative was earning tremendously. Now he felt he was earning peanuts. He came to my workshop so depressed. His problem was that he was head of a multinational bank, the number one man, but somebody got a promotion to an even higher post which he thought he deserved. He was already a number one IIM person, earning very beautifully, his wife was wonderful and so were his children.

But because somebody got a promotion which he felt he

deserved, it brought about a breakdown in him. When he was already on top with a wonderful wife and children, was an event creating a problem or his inner state? The event was that somebody got a promotion. That it registered as an impression in his mind was not a problem.

The problem was that the impression registered in the climate of anger, jealousy, hatred, ego, etc. and that climate was the inner pollution that created the problem.

So, draw the distinction between events and inner states. It is your inner state which is going to determine the quality of your life. And if that inner state is negative, it is your enemy, your *"ripuhu;"* if it is positive and really encouraging, it is your friend, your *"bandhuhu."*

The Lord says that you should work on that inner climate. To do that, we have to give ourselves some conscious, spiritual shocks. You give yourself the first spiritual shock when you see the distinction between an external event and an internal state. But this is not enough.

The second shock you have to give yourself is that you have to dis-identify yourself from the interplay of the interpreting mechanism which is polluting the impression. In the case I have just now spoken about, the impression is that somebody got a promotion – that is all. "My God, why did he get the promotion, why not me," is the interpretation.

Now, the second conscious shock you have to give yourself is that you have to push away the interpretation. The Upanishad says "neti, neti,"... not this, not this. Don't allow the inner pollution to pollute the impression, because once the impression is polluted, you perceive the other as an extension of the polluted impression.

The third conscious shock you give yourself is to develop an "emotional will" towards enlightenment and transformation, towards nirvana. An emotional will – that is when devotion (*Bhakti*) comes in. When you develop an emotional will towards enlightenment you will sacrifice life for the sake of truth. But if you live an ordinary life, you will sacrifice truth for the sake of protecting your petty life.

Look at great people's lives – they sacrifice their lives for the truth. But ordinary persons sacrifice even truth and goodness for the validation of power. You have to just look at the games which people play. For the sake of power, they sacrifice truth and goodness.

There is a very beautiful story as an example. There was a righteous and noble (*dharmik*) man, a very good and noble man. He followed truth and nothing else, but something happened to this person one day.

The god of misfortune (Shani) could not enter his house. So this god made up a strategy to enter, which was that he came in the form of a old woman to stay in that noble man's house. This righteous man could see that the woman was Shani, but still, he allowed her to come in, knowing fully well that she was the god of misfortune in disguise.

Then he found two divine lights going out of the house. He asked the lights, "Who are you?" They said, "We are *"vriddhi"* and *"siddhi"* (the gods of prosperity). "Why are you going out?" he asked. "You have allowed *"paapa,"* sin, to come inside, so we are going out," they said and went out.

Soon he found another light going out of his house and he asked, "Who are you?" The light said, "I am Lakshmi, goddess of wealth. When "*vriddhi*" and "*siddhi*" have gone I cannot exist in this house." So Lakshmi also went away. And then he found another two lights going out.

And those lights were "*satya*' and "*dharma*." When he asked, "Why are you going out," the lights said, "Lakshmi has gone, '*vriddhi*' and 'siddhi' have gone; so we, the gods of truth and righteousness, are also going away." Then this man knelt down, bowed down and cried and said, "I sacrificed my life for truth. When Lakshmi went I did not cry, when '*vriddhi*' and 'siddhi' went I did not cry, but now I cry because 'dharma' and 'satya' are going out. I allowed one sin, one 'paapa' to come in and because of that you are leaving," and he cried from the depth of his heart.

Then "*dharma*" and "*satya*" came back into the house. When they entered the house, Lakshmi also came back. He asked her, "Now why are you coming back?" She said, "Since "*dharma*" and "*satya*" have come back, I also have to come back." And then "*vriddhi*" and "*siddhi*" also came back. So the story says that where there is "*dharma*" and "*satya*" all the other gods, the "*devatas*" also exist. But it takes its own period of time.

So, you have to decide whether you are willing to give away your life for the sake of truth. But what we do is we give away truth, goodness and "*dharma*" for the sake of protecting our egos and our lives. But when absence becomes presence, you lift yourself to that truth.*

---

* Uddharet atmanaatmanam natmanam avasadayet
Atma eva atmanaha banduhu atma eva ripuhu atmanah.

Then you find that almost automatically, everything falls into place. Then a wonderful awakening happens, and you find your excellence opening up on different levels. Excellence is being absent to the ego game; our whole life is a play of ego.

The Lord says: "Ahankara vimudatma karta iti manyate;" the egoistic person is not just a fool, but a great fool. "*Moodha*" means a fool and "*vimudha*" means a great fool. The more ego you have, the more is the pressure, the tension in your being. When the ego is released there is a certain lightness of your being.

The ego is constantly demanding and playing its primitive game. You know, when you are a small child you have a certain primitive pleasure when you suck the thumb. Sucking the thumb, psychologists say, is a primitive pleasure. It is all right at that stage.

But if you are sucking the thumb at the age of, say, 14 or 15 years, it means you have not grown out of that primitive pleasure. In the spiritual paradigm the ego is a primitive pleasure. In the early stages of your life, when your "I" has to be validated, it is all right.

But when you continue to play the ego game there is so much of tension and these tensions are silent killers. You do not even know how it starts killing. If you are in the initial stage of diabetes and you go on eating sweets, it may appear as if nothing is happening to you, but for a diabetic, sweets are silent killers. Ego is also a silent killer. That is why the Lord says, "ahankara vimudhatma."

Understanding through your head is one level of understanding; understanding through feelings is another level, and understanding through your being is yet another level.

Listening itself is a great discipline or *sadhana* according to the scriptures. Listening from the mind is one level of understanding. But by listening from your heart with feeling, with devotion or *bhakti*, you get to another level of understanding, and listening from the very core of your being, from the deepest part of your being brings you to yet another level of understanding.

So first learn how to listen. Do not stop at superficial listening, the listening from the mind.

That is why the Jains call it "shravaka, shravika;" the sadhus are called *shravakas* and *shravika* is listening which itself is a certain art. So I want you to learn to listen from the level of your being. Include the listening of your mind, and include the listening of your feeling.

Let listening itself be a discipline. The word "*veda*" in Sanksrit means to know, from the word "*vid*." The other word for the Veda is "*Shruti*," which means listening. So learn to listen from your head, from your feeling, and from your being.

For example, there is a flower. If you look at a flower from your mind, you will see the chemistry of the flower. If you look at the flower from your heart, you will see the poetry of the flower. If you look at it from your being, then, like a mystic, you become the flower.

Therefore, from that perspective, listening is a great discipline. Listening is not done to collect information. Feel the words of the Gita. When you are reading the

Ramayana, you go on repeating the same thing because by repeating it you are training yourself to listen with the totality of your head, your heart and your being.

Your being void, your not being the ego, not being the "*jeevatma*," should become a presence. Your absence should become a presence. Such a presence means not having demands. I know some of you will wonder how to live life without demands. You can live life without demands, if your demands get diluted into preferences in life, and preferences are not so taxing.

I prefer silence, but if silence does not happen, I will still be in harmony with the sound. But if I demand silence, and somebody turns a page, I will get disturbed. That is the distinction. So live life with preferences rather than demands. When your presence becomes your absence, when this really happens, a lot of your tensions will come down. When tensions come down your personal excellence is going to, by default, become enhanced.

In one of my best selling books, "Oh Mind, Relax Please!," I have given this example. A bird was taking a piece of meat and flying, and all the crows went on attacking the bird. This bird did not understand why so many crows were attacking it – after all, it was only taking a piece of meat. It went up and down. It experienced tremendous struggle. Then suddenly, this bird just dropped the piece of meat. Immediately, all the crows went after the piece of meat.

The bird said, "I have lost the piece of meat, but I have discovered peace." That is why, in martial art, we say that by losing you win, and sometimes by winning you lose. In relationship also sometimes you lose, but you win peace of mind. You may win your point of view. But then what happens? You lose your peace of mind. And most of us are busy winning our point of view.

Your absence has to become your presence and your presence should be your absence. Be in harmony with what changes. Understand this clearly, with your head, your heart and your being.

Changes are happening, says the Lord, and He takes it to the peak of change, which is death. And then He says, be at peace with change. And if you are at peace with death, as a mystic beautifully said, death comes dancing to a wise person.

Because death is a new experience and you invite the new experience, you are available to it and then, even death is a wonderful phenomenon. But if you are a little more enlightened, you will see, as Lord Krishna says, that death is happening every moment.

Yesterday is gone, which is form of death and today is born and it is a form of birth. The past moment is dead and in another moment you are born. And therefore, people are upset with change because they have their dogma and opinion about what is meant by security. Drop this.

A great Indian poet once said, why are you worrying about death; when we were in the mother's womb, at that time it was the most comfortable place to be in, but at the time of delivery all of us have gone through what is called a trauma of death, because at the time of delivery the mother's womb pushes the child out.

The child has been very comfortable in the mother's womb, and the most relaxed place is the mother's womb. It is the best place and that is why in our temples the innermost shrine is called *"Garbhagudi"* – *Garbha* means womb.

But at the time of delivery, the child is pushed out of the mother's womb, and when it is pushed out it goes through the experience of death.

All of us have gone through this experience of death. The poet asked this question, were we born or did we die? We probably thought it was death, but it was a birth into the wonderful, magical, mystical, poetical world of the sun, the stars, the flora and the fauna.

So, don't be afraid of death, he says. Death is only a door to something new. A door is an empty space. Only through an empty space can there be an entry. Just imagine a house that is full of walls, built by one fellow who is very insecure that some robbers may come in there. So he has built a house with no doors and no windows. He is very secure now, but neither he nor anything else can go in.

So now the fear of insecurity has led to such a craze for security that it has become a death trap. So if there is no space, there is no entry. A door is possible only in an empty space. If it is a wall, there is no entry. Ego is like a wall. It prevents the entry of the divine.

Some people are like porcupines. If you go near, it is as if they say, "Touch me not." Some people are like walls, with frozen eyes – there is no entry allowed. And some people are like an empty space, a Chidambaram, a Chidakashaha. They are like a transparent being.

Such emptiness, such absence, is the greatest presence. You can enter only through a door, and a door can happen only in an empty space. Only if we are empty can we enter into the kingdom of God. Only then can you invite God to enter into you also.

There is a story about a barber who was an atheist and this person, his customer, who was a theist. As he was giving him a haircut the barber was saying, "I think God does not exist," and he proceeded to give the logic for it and said, "See, so much of poverty exists, so much of violence exists, if God knows all about existing beings, why does it continue to be like this."

The atheist has very great philosophy. When you analyse the atheist and the theist, in the theist there is something creative, at least he is creating the possibility of God. The atheist only negates things.

So this barber was constantly negating as he was cutting the hair. The customer remained quiet. Again, the barber said, "Because you are quiet, I think you are endorsing what I am saying." He continued to remain quiet. The barber finished the haircut and the customer went out.

In hardly three minutes he came back inside and said, "It appears there is no barber here at all." Now the barber got confused. He said, "Just now I gave you a haircut, barely three minutes back." The customer said, "When I went out of your shop, I saw so many people with long hair. That is why I said I think barbers don't exist."

The barber said, "They have to come to my shop, and then only I can cut their hair." Then this man said, "We have to invite God, only then can we eliminate ignorance, you know."

Just because there are people who have long hair, it does not mean that a barber does not exist. It is a similar foolishness to say God does not exist, because God has given you and me tremendous freedom. And our freedom is like a ladder.

With a ladder you can go up into a heaven, or you can go down into a ditch. That is the freedom the Lord has given us. So, absence must be your presence, an absence like an empty door, a Chidambara, a Chidakashaha.

15

APHORISMS FROM THE GITA HARMONISING INNER STRENGTH

f you look the whole Gita, at all the verses, it is too vast to cover one by one in a single book. So I am going to make use of the aphorism. An aphorism is like a hanger; just as on a hanger you can put so many shirts, I can hang many slokas in one aphorism.

So the aphorism I give you now is, harmonise your inner strength. This is one of the fragrances of the Gita. Many verses deal with the work of harmonising inner strength. There is inner strength in us. Hanuman had tremendous strength, but he was not confident of it.

The moment he harmonised and locked into his inner strength, you know what all he did in the Ramayana. So the Gita tells us to harmonise our inner strength. And this harmonising is done through the principle of yoga. Yoga is one discipline, the principle of Vedanta is another discipline. Lord Krishna speaks of yoga in the Gita, which is helpful for our personal excellence; he mentions also the Vedanta.

The discipline (*anushasana*) of yoga is to learn to harmonise. Now, what is it that you have to harmonise?

There are four locks – there is a body lock, an emotional lock, an intellectual lock, and a spiritual lock.

When you perform a "*havan*," (fire ritual) what happens is the fire that is locked in the wood is released. That is why in the traditional way two pieces of wood are taken and rubbed to light the fire; it is not done with the match stick. The fire is locked in the wood, and by rubbing two bits of wood you get a fire, and from this the fire of the "*havan*" is lit. Hindu monks wear fire-coloured dress to signify that the fire of knowledge is in us, as the fire is in the wood, but it has to be rubbed to make it come out.

Similarly, knowledge and intelligence in the body, in your emotion, in your intellect, in your spiritual centre, are all there, all four of them, but it is like the fire in the wood. You have to rub it, and the equivalent of such rubbing is to do "*mananam*," By "*mananam*," (reflection) you have to bring out the fire of knowledge to dispel ignorance.

A part of your personal excellence is to understand the intelligence in your body. That is why, if you want to be a body builder, you train your body to build up muscles. If you want to be a karate expert, you train your body to create in it karate intelligence. If you are a hockey player, or a basketball player, you train your body to have the skill to navigate and dribble the ball. Therefore, the need for the training of the body, is to unlock the lock.

What is the lock you should unlock? I will put it in a simple nutshell and you will understand so long as you are not a nut. The simple way of explaining is called the grapes (*draksha phalam*) style.

There are three different styles of literature – "*draksha*

phalam," "nari phalam," and *"kadali phalam." "Nari phalam"* is the coconut; you have to break the coconut to get the water. Some styles of literature are such you have to break your head to understand what the author is saying, because the sentence starts here and ends after three pages.

The second style of literature is the *"kadali phalam"* – you don't have to put in very great effort to peel the plantain. You have to put in a little effort, "alpa prayatnam," and you can eat the fruit. Kalidasa's works are in this style.

The third style is "draksha phalam," which means the grape style, needing no effort; just open your mouth, and pop it inside.

Now I have to improvise in the *"draksha phalam"* style, because in Kaliyuga mouths open only for pizza and burger. So what do I do? I crack jokes, make it humourous, then they open their mouths to laugh and then I push the Vedanta inside. And still, some people don't laugh when I crack jokes.

I want you to know that the Bhagavad Gita is a book not only for students, but even for teachers. And every parent should be a student and a teacher.

The beauty of the Bhagavad Gita is that it is a book for teachers and students, because the styles of teaching, both the soft and the hard techniques are given.

The Lord at times was hard to Arjuna and sometimes soft too. Good parenting and good teaching must be soft and they must also be hard. In the art of war also, sometimes the hard technique is used and sometimes it is the soft one. I want you to understand all these very clearly.

I like to use the grandmother's tactics.

See how a grandmother feeds her grandchild. She says, "What is that on the top of the tree?"

The child says, "Crow!"

"What does the crow say?" she asks.

The child says, "Ka, ka!" and opens its mouth, and then some idli is quickly stuffed inside.

This is exactly what I am doing. I am cracking some jokes and then pushing Vedanta inside, or else the child does not eat the idli. I crack a joke to entertain you, to make you open your mind, and then I put enlightenment inside. That is why teaching is a great art.

So I am putting this in a very simple "draksha phalam" (grape) style. There is a body lock, all of you can understand this. If you are going to eat pizza for breakfast, burger for lunch, 10 masala dosas for your snack-time, the whole body lock will get drowned inside.

So what you have to do is open up your body lock. Good exercises, good breathing and moderate eating – "Yukta ahara viharasya," as the Lord says. He goes into these details about how your "ahara," your food should be moderate, your "vihara," your activity also should be moderate, because it should not lead to leakage of energy.

You should be active in such a way that you store energy and don't leak it away. For your personal excellence, this is a great message.

When I am giving a discourse, my talking, which is my action, should deepen my silence, and my silence should deepen my action. If I have to hit a nail into the wall, I have to use 5 units of strength from my wrist ... that is all.

But some people will use their whole body including the thighs to hit a small nail.

This is called leakage of energy. The economy of action is to store energy. Put in only the effort which is required to hit the nail in the wall, and you store energy. Your personal excellence will be tremendously enhanced.

Now, what is music? Music is just not sound. It is the gap between the sounds that creates music. Only sound does not create music. When sounds are put in harmony it is music, and what is harmony? It is the silence between two sounds. And the silence between two sounds creates depth to the sound, which in turn adds depth to silence.

So silence and sounds start interplaying with each other and create a symphony. I leave it at this for you to think over.

Action should store energy rather than leak energy. And the whole science of yoga gets into this. Your personal excellence will happen when you do this.

So, in a simple nutshell, the body centre has a positive and a negative energy. If you are using more energy than required to while talking it is a negative energy. If you are sitting down and shaking your legs unnecessarily there is a leakage of energy.

Have you seen some people talking into a mike? They will shout as if the mike does not exist and that energy is more than what is required. I have seen it in the way some people move their bodies also. It is not required. Some people have this problem even when they chant mantras. They have not learnt the knack.

When you play tennis, when you squeeze the racket too much, there is a leakage of energy. When you hit the ball, and the ball goes, then you should quickly transfer it to the left hand and loosen the grip as you run. When the ball comes back, hold the racket with a good grip. Only when you hit the ball you squeeze the racket to hit.

In the initial period when you play tennis, you hold the racket as though it is disappearing from you; actually it is the ball that disappears. If you squeeze the racket too much, the racket will not disappear, but the ball will disappear. When the ball disappears the score comes down.

Therefore the body energy is very important. The body lock opens up when you are relaxed. There is positive energy and there is negative energy. If there is leakage of energy it is negative. If there is storage of energy it is positive.

In your emotional centre too, there are positive and negative energies. You look at somebody and you get jealous. With jealousy, emotional drainage happens. You see somebody happy and then you become unhappy because you think, "How come the rascal is happy when I am unhappy?"

Unnecessarily, emotional leakage happens. In intellectual energy also, there is the positive, and there is the negative. The whole intellectual acumen of some people is used to prove that God does not exist. What is achieved by that? Nothing – the theist, by creating a concept of God, at least creates hope.

The atheist does not create hope, and he becomes hopeless. Therefore your intellect also can be positive or negative. So the body is positive or negative, the emotion is positive or negative, the intellect is positive or negative, and your whole sense of being is also positive or negative.

If you can renounce the negative, and align the positive together, a synergy happens, and in the synergy a magnetic centre opens up. When the magnetic centre opens up, you become a cup that the rain from heaven can fill. But most of the time our physical, emotional, intellectual and spiritual cups are positioned upside down, so even when God's blessings come, the cup is not in a right posture to receive.

Through Hatha yoga, the body learns to store energy and not leak it out; through Bhakti yoga, there is storage of emotional energy, not leakage; through Gnana yoga there is storage of intellectual energy and not leakage, and through Dhyana yoga there is storage of spiritual energy, not leakage. When the positives of these four align together – your internal cup, the internal receptor, opens up to the possibility of life.

When it is open to the possibility of life and the rain of blessing happens, you can really absorb it. It has to be a positive strength. Hitler had tremendous emotional strength. He himself was not a German, he was an Austrian. But he could move Germany to hate Jews. So that was a negative strength. When you harmonise your inner strength make sure it is a positive strength.

"What should I do in order to be enlightened?" asked the student of the master. The master replied, "As much as you can do to make the sun rise and the sun set." "Then what is the use of all the spiritual practices?" said the student. "Only to make sure," the master said, "that you are awake when the sun rises, and you are awake when the sun sets."

To be awake, your inner receptor should open. Throughout the Gita, the Lord says have detachment (*vairagya*) with regard to your negative currents and have a sense of commitment towards your positive currents. And this discipline of harmonising your inner strength positively is an aphorism for your personal excellence. Many of the verses deal with that.

Please work on this. When you are cooking your food, you do it with full tension in the body. You take the frying pan, squeezing it as though you are squeezing the body energy.

Then, emotionally, you are in full tension, you curse, "Oh my misfortune, why did I marry my husband, I should have waited a little more, his uncle was better," and so, emotional leakage. "Why have I been such an idiot, I think it is a manufacturer's defect," you think, and there is leakage of intellectual energy there, so you are cooking your food with full leakage of energy.

Likewise, people who have to go the airport, they are relaxing till the last minute and then in unnecessary tension they quickly dress up. You should plan it out, and not do this. And therefore, harmonising inner strength is a very important aphorism in the Gita for your personal excellence.

B. DRAW YOUR ENERGY FROM YOUR INNER STRENGTH

Sukhaduhkhe same krtva labhalabhau jaya jayau
Tato yuddhaya yujya sva naivam papamavapsyasi.

I will use the sloka as a trigger and connect and log on to many other slokas in the Gita. "Sukha dukhe same krtva" – learn to be calm and open always.

Here is another aphorism for you to develop personal excellence, especially in Gita-oriented management. The aphorism has the quintessence of the Gita, which is:

"Keep your sorrow in silence, draw your energy from your internal strength and go with the flow."

We are like the football which is kicked by players, and most of them, like the football, are kicked by situations of life.

The kicking may be whatever – the boss may scold you, you may not understand your guru, somebody gets a promotion which you deserve, your wife has cheated on you, your husband has cheated on you – all these become conflict and sorrow situations.

So, we start worrying. Worrying becomes a habit and then when you start worrying, this one worry thought triggers off or stimulates or hooks on to the past unhappy thought. The past unhappy thought triggers another unhappy thought, and another unhappy thought logs on another unhappy thought. And then under this avalanche you start collapsing.

Have you seen the arguments of husband and wife? "Don't be like your mother," she says, meaning, don't be adamant like your mother. "Don't insult me," he says. She says, "I am not insulting you, don't be like your mother."

He says, "You are insulting me, my boss also insulted me, my grandmother also insulted me, my neighbour also insulted me!" The word "insult" triggers off all that insults that you have gone through in the past, it has a chain effect, a reactive effect, it keeps logging on till it becomes an avalanche that makes you collapse.

In what started as a simple conversation between husband and wife, you have logged on to your hurt-bank account, on to all the fixed deposits you have collected, and you are crushed by your own currency of misery.

You have to catch how your mind works. Please understand that whenever you are unhappy, whenever you are hurt, if you don't control the effort there itself, the hurt, like a virus, will enter into yet another file of your past, and go into your childhood upsets also. Then your system will crash. So then, how can personal excellence happen?

Therefore, keep your sorrow in silence; just calm down, chant "Ram, Ram," or the Gayatri mantra, they are all calming techniques. So when you are upset, just calm yourself, keep your upset in silence, and understand that the upset is nothing but a movement of thoughts. An event exists in you as an impression. Impressions are more real than events.

But the impression gets polluted, by the polluting factors we have already dwelt on.

Somebody calls you an idiot, you are upset, and this upset is a movement of thought. When there is a movement of thought what happens is that we see the object of thoughts and not the subject of thoughts. That is the biggest mistake in life. The object of the thought is the other person who has upset you.

A meditator will look at the subject of the thought. Thought exists in space. But before the thought comes there was space, because thought exists in psychological space. The same thought goes away, but the inner space continues to exist. A hall is a space which was there before you came in, and is there when you are also there, and continues to be there when you go away.

So also, before you were hurt there was that thought-space, when you are hurt also there is that space, so when you really look at that space, you see the subject of thought. Unfortunately, we don't look, but if you do, you will see that the subject of thought is silence, is Chidambaram. That is why philosophy is called "Darshan Sastra," it is about looking. So the subject of thought is silence, and when you log on to the silence instead of logging on to the object of thought then you find that the thought slowly disappears.

Like a tennis player who logs on only to the ball, you log on to silence. When a disturbing thought happens, *"same krtva,"* be calm and instead of seeing the object of thought, look at the space in which thought exists, and that space is silence, so log on to the silence. But what we do when the thought comes is we add our internal chaos to it.

Therefore, keep your sorrow in silence. We don't do that; we justify our sorrow, we curse it, we get angry with it, we say life is being too cruel to me, or that rascal is always doing this to me.

We are in the object of thought or the justifying mood. We are not in silence, and for the meditator the practice is that whenever you feel disturbed, whatever the disturbances be, don't look at the object, look at the subject.

Keep your sorrow in your silence, draw your energy from your inner strength; this is the aphorism I have derived from this sloka and several others (it is not the translation). The inner strength is silence, in which thought exists; your inner strength is a commitment to be a part of solution, it is your belief that life is a possibility rather than a sheer ego game.

Like Hanuman, log on to inner strength. We draw our energy from worry and from ego. The Gita says draw your energy from the inner strength. And the greatest inner strength is the power to be silent, the power to be calm.

For that to happen, you have to have the strength of a deep belief. Lord Krishna says, "Shraddhavaan labhate gnanam." The one who has faith achieves knowledge. The greatest decision you have to take is to decide to choose a right belief.

Why? One's belief creates a reality. It is like the placebo effect. If you have a stomach ache the doctor gives you dud tablets and he says that it will remove your stomach ache. You take it believing it is a medicine for your stomach ache and it disappears.

This is called the placebo effect. In the placebo effect what has healed you? Not the dud tablet, but the belief, because belief creates reality.

So the Lord says that *"shraddha"* creates. When I say keep the sorrow in silence and draw your energy from your internal strength, the internal strength is silence, commitment, and belief.

Have a deep belief that you are going to be enlightened. Have a deep belief that you are going to be successful, that you have to be a part of the solution, rather than a victim to your problem. People listen to the discourse, but their belief is that in this birth they will never be enlightened. And the belief creates reality.

Look at the life history of successful people. Beethoven was deaf when he was composing his masterpiece. Stephen Hawking cannot even speak, he has a voice modulator, but he is one of the greatest scientists the world has ever produced.

In my books I have given umpteen examples. Such people are physically challenged but psychologically they have a tremendous belief system. "Main to hoon vishwas mein;" Saint Kabir says that God says, "I am in your belief." So believe deeply that the Lord's blessings are there, that you will be enlightened, that the best things will happen to you.

When you have these deep beliefs, everything will be good; you will experience a magical silence.

A Sufi Fakir was in love with a girl. After 15 years of waiting, their families accepted the match, and they got married, and immediately boarded a boat to sail to his house on the other shore.

Suddenly, there was a great storm the boat seemed about to sink, but the Sufi mystic was very relaxed. The wife said, "Are you not scared that you are going to die?"

And the Sufi mystic said, "No." "What is the reason," said the wife.

He took out his knife, pointed it at his wife and said, "I am going to kill you. Are you scared?" And she said, "No." "Why not?" he asked.

She said," The knife may be dangerous, but the one who is holding the knife loves me very much. He has loved me for 15 years, so I am not scared."

And the Sufi mystic said, "The waves may be dangerous, but Allah, who controls the waves loves me very much. Therefore I am not scared."

The best things will happen, when you have belief. Something beyond logic and energy happens. So this is internal strength. So keep your sorrow in silence, draw your energy from your internal strength, and go with the flow.

Look at Lord Krishna's life – He flows with life. He can dance with the Gopis, He can be a kshatriya, He can also just be a charioteer without a weapon in a area full of weapons. In all conditions, like water, Krishna can flow through them. The art of flowing with what is and not fighting with it is what a kshatriya should know, is what He tells Arjuna.

Martial art teaches you how to flow with your enemy. And when you flow with the enemy you can successfully attack him. Martial art is a demonstration of that. Tai chi is about flowing movements.

If you flow as somebody attacks you, you can use that person's energy and throw him off. That is why the word Judo means the way of gentleness. Karate means with an empty hand. Both can be very spiritual. The martial arts basically come from India, from Kerala. Therefore, go with the flow. Don't fight it.

One of the wonderful experiences I have had happened when one of my workshops in San Francisco was cancelled and my students very lovingly took me to Hawaii.

There, I was with one of my organisers, a Muslim lady who conducts Mantra Yoga, and a local Hawaiian who was my brother's friend taught me how to float. I knew how to float in a swimming pool. I did not know how to float in the ocean. Floating is a knack. He taught me how to float, and I was floating beautifully. Then I said, "My hostess has been working so hard for our workshops, teach her how to float, but she does not know swimming."

And the local Hawaiian said to her, "You need not know swimming, the ocean holds you from below, the waves just keep coming," and slowly he left her hand and she started floating. For nearly 10 minutes she was floating, and the huge waves were coming, and I said to this man, "She does not know to swim and the waves are coming," and this man said, "Swamiji, you have written "Oh Mind, Relax Please!," so please relax." When I get advice from a student I love it. They show me so much of love. And then I saw that she had closed her eyes, and there was a huge wave, and she was not aware of this, and the huge wave just took her up with itself.

Then he told me, "If you fight with the waves you drown, if you don't fight you can float with the wave. Dead people don't drown because they don't fight, people who are alive fight, and therefore drown." The ability to float with life is a tremendous piece of personal excellence.

This is what the sloka, "Sukhaduhkhe same krtva labhalabhau jayajayau," is about; float with your gain and your loss. Then you will never create any conflict or any sin, "naivam papamavapsyasi," because sin is not being in harmony with life. Sin is when you are against life. Lord Krishna does not want us to be against life. He wants us to flow with it. You will understand this only if you are very calm and serene.

So get this aphorism. Keep your sorrow in silence, don't go to the object of sorrow, go to the subject of sorrow, your thought-space, where there is silence; be calm, draw your energy, not from worries but from internal strength, which is nourished by your belief, and go with the flow. It is something you have to practice. This is true of any knowledge or "vidya".

When you are learning music, initially, you get it and yet you have not got it. You have to pass through that phase. If you get tensed about it, you cannot go further. Float with life. And when you do, personal excellence will garland your every moment. You will dance with the moment.

C. OUR CAPABILITIES ARE BEYOND OUR LIMITATIONS

Yavanartha udapane sarvatah samplutodake
Tavansarveshu vedesu brahmanasya vijanataha.
(Chapter II, sloka 46)

This sloka connects to many slokas of the Gita in a simple aphorism: your capabilities are beyond limitations. The problem with us is that we log on to and connect to our limitations. If there is a limitation of your body, you connect to that limitation, if there is a limitation of your emotion you connect to that, if there is a limitation of your mind you connect to that.

But you must understand that your capabilities are beyond your limitations; that is why the Veda says "Aham Brahmasmi" – you are infinite. Though the body has limitations and the mind has limitations, our essence is infinite, so life exists as an interplay between the infinite and finite.

Adi Shankaracharya says, whether you are in yoga or in *bhoga*, in the midst of people or a recluse, you are not affected by either condition because you are infinite.

Further, the infinite can never be other than finite. If infinite is other than finite, it is finite, not infinite. Infinite is in spite of finite. To give another example, freedom is not other than bondage. If freedom is other than bondage, then it is bound by freedom, for it is free in freedom and not free in bondage. Therefore freedom is bound by itself.

So freedom is not other than bondage. Freedom is in spite of bondage.

Stephen Hawking has the limitations of being physically challenged, but what great possibilities as well. Beethoven was deaf when he composed his greatest music. Helen Keller also had great limitations, but she was such a great person. Thomas Alva Edison, who was half deaf, was one of the greatest scientists. O. J. Simpson suffered from an ailment called rickets, but he became one of the greatest American football players of all time.

All of them had limitations, but their capabilities existed with the same limitations, like how freedom includes bondage, and it is not other than bondage. So freedom is not in conflict with bondage. Therefore, be in harmony with conflict and not in conflict with harmony.

Somebody went to great martial art expert Bruce Lee and asked him, "Can you teach me martial art?" This man was already a black belt. His name was Mr. Joe. Bruce Lee asked, "Are you willing to drop what you have learnt?" He asked, "Is what I have learnt something bad?" Bruce Lee said, "What you have learnt is not bad, but to learn you must be willing to drop what you have learnt."

He then explained with a beautiful Zen example. Somebody went to the Zen Master to defeat him in a discussion. And the Zen master said, "Have a cup of tea." He started pouring into an empty cup, and the cup became full but he continued pouring and it started overflowing. And that man said, "What are you doing? It is overflowing." The Zen master said, "Your mind is a cup already filled, if I pour into it, it will overflow." And Bruce

Lee said, "This is what I am saying."

Then the man said, "I am willing to drop what I have learnt," and Bruce Lee began to teach him. Then the student said, "I don't think I will be able to learn. When I have to give kicks on the face, my legs are not going up to the face because I am 50 years old."

Bruce Lee said, "Why try to hit the head, the chest is the broader target." And then he said, "I don't think I have the perfect body to fight." Bruce Lee said, "I also don't have a perfect body. My right leg is roughly an inch shorter than my left, and that is why I will put my right leg forward in my stance."

If anybody sees Bruce Lee in action he will say, "What a perfect body he has!" He converted his limitation into strength. You think you have limitations, but again your capabilities are beyond your limitations.

Still this man was not convinced, just as some of you are not convinced.

Then Bruce Lee said, "I will tell you one more thing which nobody knows – I am short sighted. Therefore, my specialisation is the close encounter. I have converted my disadvantage into an advantage. Also, I do not know English well, but I am the first Chinese who was invited to Hollywood."

We are much more than what we think we are.

In our lives, finite and infinite play with each other, bondage and freedom dance with each other; the Ying and the Yang, the sound and the silence, play with each other.

Sound is opposed to silence. But in music, sound and

silence play together and silence gives music to sound and sound gives magic to silence. And therefore, you and I listen to the symphony of music.

If you continue breathing in, without exhaling, breathing in will suffocate you. Breathing in is the opposite of breathing out, but the breathing in helps you to breathe out and breathing out helps you to breathe in. Similarly, limitations and capabilities play against each other, although in the structure of logical thinking it appears as if the opposites displace each other.

We focus on our limitations, but our capabilities go beyond limitations. This is what the Lord unfolds in the verse:

Yavanartha udapane sarvatah samplutodake
Tavansarveshu vedesu brahmanasya vijanataha.

Right near the ocean, on the beach, if you dig, you can take out one mug of water for cleaning yourself. But that small well is flooded with oceanic water and with that small pot you can take the water of the ocean itself. Once you know this, once you have this vision that your infinite includes the finite, a different skill begins to happen.

Your limitations become ineffective when you log on your capabilities, which are beyond limitations. The problem with our logical thinking is we think the infinite is the opposite of finite.

I came across a very rare Sanskrit book. One of my students gave me this book. If you read the slokas from left to right it is the Ramayana; if you read them from right to left it becomes the Bhagavata. It is a masterpiece.

Look at the capabilities. I am sure the author, who is from Andhra Pradesh, had limitations, but he has written 40 verses like this. I am breaking my head to understand the meaning. Such scholars were supported by kings. Without support, they all disappear.

Even this great author had limitations. But his capabilities were beyond limitations. Log on to this inspirational happening. And when you log on and when you come from that belief system, a different kind of possibility happens.

D. LOOK LESS SEE MORE

The ability to see *"what is as is"* is an important dimension of seeing. The way we look is very important, the way we see is important. The problem with us is that we don't see.

A lady came to me and said, "I feel extremely lonely, what should I do?" Her husband is a great artist and she is feeling lonely.

I said, "You have to learn how to see and not simply look. Learn how to see from your husband; he is a famous artist and artists look at a flower from different angles, and feel they are seeing many flowers. Sometimes he sees the structure of beauty in a way he never imagined, and he realises that he has been looking but not seeing. You have to learn to see."

"See what?" she said.

I said, "See the stars, the moon, the flora and the fauna. Even look at your dog honestly. Ask your husband about this, he will endorse it.

"I have spoken on the Bhagavad Gita many times, but every time, I look at it from a different angle, and something new happens. Ask the musician, he takes the same raga – musical notes – and does the *'alap'* in different ways and he will say, 'My God, this piece is so beautiful.' The problem with you is you are not able to see."

She said, "I am looking."

I said, "You are looking through the lenses of your ego, you are looking through the lenses of desire (kama), anger (krodha), greed (lobha), attachment (moha), arrogance (mada), matsarya (jealousy), so you are looking more but seeing less."

When we look at people, we look not only through (kama), anger (krodha), greed (lobha), attachment (moha), arrogance (mada), matsarya (jealousy), but also through the conditioning of a Brahmin, of a Kshatriya, or a Vyshya, or the conditioning of a Christian, or a Muslim. When we look at life through those lenses, we look more but see less. Lord Krishna says remove all those lenses, and look with innocence. And then only, you look less and see more.

Therefore, in the Gita, another important point is:

Nirdvandvo hi mahabaho sukham bandhatpramucyate

Krishna says, "Drop your *dwandvas*, your lenses of liking (raga) and disliking (dwesha), of (kama), anger (krodha), greed (lobha), attachment (moha), arrogance (mada), matsarya (jealousy), free yourself and then see how easily you get liberated, O Arjuna."

When you are seeing the flower, just see. Change the angle of your seeing and you see something unique. With that simple seeing, see the flower blooming, see at the birds flying, and you will find an aesthetic seeing happens.

E. PERSONAL EFFECTIVENESS

More than the slokas of the Gita, if you look at Lord Krishna's life, you will see how it gives you techniques for personal effectiveness.

There is a beautiful story in the Mahabharata which depicts this. There was a wild cat and there was a rat. The cat was after the rat. The rat entered into the hole and the cat was waiting outside, because the rat was inside the hole.

Who will win? It all depends on who is more alert, because God has given intelligence to both the rat and the cat.

The cat got tired of waiting, and started going away. As he was going away, he got caught in the hunter's net. He began to struggle, and the rat heard the noise. The rat came out with confidence. The cat was caught and helpless in the net and the rat was going away, when it found there was a huge bird coming towards it, but it was quite some distance to go to the hole, so the bird was likely to pick up the rat.

Immediately, the rat got an idea and negotiated with the cat. "If you save me I will save you," It said. How? "The bird is coming to get me, so I will come inside the net with you and you save me. And if you save me I will go out and cut the net." The cat got confused with the courage of the rat and agreed. And the rat got inside the net and sat on the lap of the cat. The bird could not do anything and went away.

Then the cat realised that now if I don't allow the rat to

leave, I cannot get out and the hunter is coming soon. If I eat the rat the hunter will finish me. So he let the rat go. The rat also saw the hunter coming, but the hunter could not see the cat and rat.

The rat went round the net and slightly cut the bits of the net, and the cat got restless and said, "Hurry up, the hunter is coming." The rat said, "Don't worry, I will honour my word. When I will honour it, I will not tell. I said I will cut the net. When I will cut it I, will not tell you now."

So the rat cuts a little and goes around twice, doing *pradakshinas*, then cuts a little more and does four rounds of *pradakshinas*. The cat now is in tension and yelling, "You are cheating me." The rat says, "No, I am not." By the time the hunter came very close there was only one strand left and immediately, the rat cut the strand, the cat came out and the rat ran to the hole and cat ran for its life. When the hunter came he could not see anything.

Then there was a dialogue. The daughter rat asked, "Mummy, why were you so slow in cutting the net?" And the mother said, "Because I am not stupid like Daddy. If I'd cut the net too fast, the cat would have eaten me. I had to honour my word, but the cat will not change."

So people hardly change, but at the same time you might have to support the enemy also. We keep a distance from the enemy so that we don't get cheated by him. Look at Lord Krishna's life. He always honoured his word.

So firstly, in life you have to honour your word. Secondly, help even your enemy. Thirdly, understand that people rarely change. Even in spirituality, they change superficially.

I have told you already about two conscious shocks. We usually don't give ourselves the third conscious shock. Therefore, we don't change.

So honour your word, be useful to your enemy, and understand that people rarely change, and even when they do, they change superficially, so you have to be close to your enemy and yet create a distance from him. Lord Krishna was not only intelligent, but he was tactful. In life, what we have to learn from Lord Krishna is that being very knowledgeable is not enough; you also have to learn to be tactful.

One lady came to me and said, "Swamiji, I tried my best to change my husband but he has not changed." I asked, "What is the problem?" She said, "He comes home at 2 o'clock in the night. I have been so truthful but it has not worked." People hardly change because they are not willing to give themselves a third shock.

So I gave her a strategy, I taught her tact and the tact worked very well. Let us say her husband's name was Sharma. As he came into the room at 2 a.m., the sleeping wife mumbled, "Hey Kuppuswamy, have you come?" Kuppuswamy was the neighbour. From that day, the husband stopped coming late. Therefore, you should be tactful also in life. Not cunning, but tactful. Lord Krishna is tactful, like Chanakya.

When you can learn to be calm, drawing energy from internal strength, one sickening question you will not ask is, "Why me?" There is this wonderful true incident in the life of Arthur Ashe, the Wimbledon champion who died of AIDS.

Somebody asked him, "Don't you ask the question, why me?"

Arthur Ashe said, "There are billions of people on this earth, of whom a few millions are learning tennis, and out of this, say, some ten thousand people are going into professional sports, and out of these, maybe a thousand people come into international sports, out of whom only 30 get selected for Wimbledon, and out of this 30, only 8 people come into the semi-finals, and then only two people are in the finals, and I was one of the two and I won.

"At that time I never asked God, 'Why me?' So now why should I ask God, 'Why me?'"

When you live a full life, you never ask the question, "Why me?" You go with the flow. Lord Krishna's life was so full – he was a warrior, he was playful, he was intense, he was relaxed, he was both Ying and Yang, Male and Female energy, his life had *anandalahari, premalahari, soundaryalahari,* everything. He was multi-dimensional and full, because he was fully in the moment, whether it was perfect or imperfect.

My brother is a Yoga teacher in Brascia near Milano. Many years ago, he called me to his place and when I went to Zurich for my workshop, I went there. I attended all his yoga classes, and all his students were local Italians, who hardly knew any English, and he was taking yoga classes, talking in Italian.

I was literally zapped, because he had gone just two years back and now had picked up such good Italian while I am still struggling with Indian languages, though academically I am more brilliant than him. I felt utterly confused. Back at his home, I said in amazement, in *"adhbhuta* (wonderment) *rasa,"* that he had picked up Italian so well, but was it correct Italian, I asked him.

He said, "Correct or not I have not bothered, but I am enjoying my Italian, and they are doing yoga correctly. In fact, I don't want to improve my Italian because that is my unique selling point. Nobody can talk like me, but everybody can talk like them." You can be complete in your imperfection also. If you enjoy what you are doing like he was enjoying his own style of speaking Italian, then one becomes complete.

Be complete, see the beauty. If your husband leaves you it does not matter, if you are lonely, enjoy the loneliness, then you can see the beauty of being away from that horrible man.

There is beauty in imperfection. If you cannot see beauty in imperfection, then you will get tense, and personal excellence can never happen by tension.

A young girl went to a psychiatrist and said, "I have tremendous tension." The psychiatrist hugged her, kissed her and sat down. "Why did you do that?" the young girl asked. The psychiatrist said, "I relieved my tension, now tell me about your tension."

Lord Krishna never collected tension, nor did he go around kissing people. The point is that if you cannot see beauty in what is, in imperfection, you unnecessarily get tense. And when you get tense, your personal excellence will not flow.

Take my brother's example, he is imperfect in Italian yet

so comfortable in it, and he loves his imperfection. Love your imperfection. Then *"samsara"* is not going to be a problem. *"Samsara"* is so wonderful that it is itself a nirvana. Lord Krishna's life is a depiction of that. Some people who are interested in nirvana sit for 10 days meditation with full tension. What comes out of such meditation is only tension.

Learn to love your ignorance also. Then your ignorance has a lustre. Lord Krishna's life is a depiction of lustre, and *"anandalahari," "premalahari,"* and *"soundaryalahari"* are the essence of Lord Krishna's life.

I have explained some concepts – create a harmony in conflict, bring flexibility in strength and strength in flexibility. I have talked of male energy and female energy, commitment and acceptance. But sometimes in my teaching I leave certain things vague because I want you to think.

That is where your psychological collaterals and bridges have to be built. Very few are using the grand prerogative of mind. Those who never really think, think they do. Therefore, if some parts of the teachings of Vedanta sometimes go a little above your head, it is a chance for you to realize you do have a head.

A section of large crowd during Gita Talks by Swamiji

Two views of Prasanna Centre for Life Management

51, Ground Floor, 16th Cross,
Between 6th & 8th Main
Malleswaram, Bangalore 560 055, India
Tel: +91 80 4153 5832-35
Fax: +91 80 23444112
E-Mail: prasannatrust@vsnl.com
www.swamisukhabodhananda.org
www.prasannatrust.org
www.ohmindrelaxplease.org

Prasanna Trust is a registered social charitable trust set up with the objective to re-look at various facets of Indian philosophy and culture for effective transformation of individuals in particular and the society in general.

We have made our presence primarily through :

- Transformative Education

- Social Oriented Service

TRANSFORMATIVE EDUCATION

a) LIFE – LIVING IN FREEDOM – AN ENQUIRY

It is a 2 days workshop on personal effectiveness through interactions and meditations. An experience oriented, non-religious program designed to enhance productivity, handling stress, personal well-being and organisational synergy. It focuses on bringing forth the outer winner leading to creativity and an inner winner to meditative consciousness.

b) EXISTENTIAL LABORATORY

It is a 4-days residential retreat set amidst natural surroundings to experience oneself through a series of dynamic and passive meditations in order to see connectivity with nature, to heal and release the inner child, to realise innocence and wonderment in all walks of life based on the Upanishad truths – Chakshumathi Vidya.

c) CORPORATE HARMONY AND CREATIVITY
It is a 2 days comprehensive workshop for senior level executives to harness creativity and harmony in today's competitive work environment and preparing them for globalisation.

d) YOUTH PROGRAMME
It is a 3 days program based on multiple intelligence. The program develops the hidden talent and skill in a child; to enable the child to face the world with confidence as each child is unique.

e) OH, MIND RELAX PLEASE!
It is a 1 day seminar based on unique techniques to transform from ordinary to extra-ordinary, dealing with fear and conflicts and converting them as challenges.

f) RELATIONSHIP MATRIX SEMINAR
An exclusive workshop to discover alchemy of different spectrum of relationship, be it father, mother, spouse, children, sibblings, boss, subordinate colleagues, associate peers..., so as to discover togetherness in a relationship.

g) TEACHERS' TRAINING PROGRAMME
A 5 days workshop designed to train and develop an individual as Pracharak or teacher for spreading the universal message for the benefit of society.

h) MANTRA YOGA PROGRAMME – A Holistic approach to Life
A workshop based on five powerful Mantras to help in enhancing health, unlocking the blissful centre, increasing intuitive ability, creating wealth and divinity in oneself and others. This program is conducted in English and also in many Indian languages by well trained Pracharaks.

i) NIRGUNA MANDIR – A Meditation Centre for Learning

* Unfolding the traditional texts of the Bhagavad Gita & the Upanishads as is relevant in today's living context.
* Workshops to bring forth creativity and awareness among youth, women and parents through a spiritual paradigm.
* Research to foster universal love through an interreligious forum.
* Orientation programs for trainers and social workers.
* Spiritual inputs to deal with phobia, fear, trauma, drug and alcoholic abuse.

SOCIAL ORIENTED SERVICE

a) CHILD CARE CENTRE – A HOME FOR HOMELESS - PRASANNA JYOTHI:
Nurturing lives of little angels who have been orphaned due to the paradox of circumstances. Uncared girls who otherwise would have withered away are growing into enthusiastic, intelligent, celebrative and responsible children.

b) VOCATIONAL TRAINING FOR CHILDREN:
In order to keep abreast with the fast changing face of the world, it is proposed to give the children of Prasanna Jyothi training in office automation & allied area of skills.

We seek support of individuals, business houses, institutions and invite them to be part of this noble vision of creating an atmosphere to impart our culture and thus contributing to the society we build.

*Contribution to **Prasanna Trust** account is exempted from Income Tax under Section 80 (G)*

TITLES OF SWAMIJI'S WORKS

BOOKS

Meditation *(from Bhagavad Gita) (also in Kannada, Tamil, Telugu & Hindi)*

Karma Yoga *(based on Bhagavad Gita)*

Wisdom through Silence
(Commentary on Dhakshina Murthy Stotram)

Oh, Life Relax Please!
(also in Hindi, Tamil, Telugu, Kannada, Gujarati and Marati)

Oh, Mind Relax Please!
(also in Tamil, Telugu, Kannada, Malayalam, Hindi, Marati & Gujarati)

Oh, Mind Relax Please! – Part 2
(only in Tamil, Kannada & Telugu)

Looking Life Differently *(also in Tamil Telugu, Kannada & Hindi)*

Wordless Wisdom *(also in Tamil, Kannada, Hindi & Telugu)*

Stress Management – A bullet proof Yogic Approach *(also in Kannada)*

Art of Wise Parenting *(also in Kannada)*

Agame Relax Please! *(in Tamil)*

Kutumbave Relax Please! *(in Kannada & Telugu)*

Golden Words for Good Living

Roar Your Way to Excellence *(also in Kannada)*

Celebrating Success & Failure *(also in Kannada)*

Harmonising Inner Strength

AUDIO
TRADITIONAL UNFOLDMENT

Gayatri Mantra *(also in regional languages)*
Maha Mruthyunjaya Mantra *(also in regional languages)*
Om Gam Ganapate Namaha *(also in regional languages)*
Om Krishnaya Namaha *(also in regional languages)*
Om Shivaya Namaha *(also in regional languages)*
Mantra Chants
Trataka Yogic Technique
Shiva Sutras
Essence of Bhagavad Gita
Guru Purnima

MEDITATION

Brahmayagna

Navratri Upasana

Bhakti Yoga

Mantra Healing

Maha Visarjana Kriya

Meditation, the Music of Silence

Vedic Vision to Pregnant women

Yoga Laya

OCCULT TEACHINGS

Seven Chakras of Hindu Psychology
Symbolism of Hindu Rituals
Essence of Hinduism
Who am I?
Healing Hurt through Gayatri Mantra
Handling insecurity through Mruthyunjaya Mantra
Handling crisis through Taraka Mantra

MANAGEMENT –
A NEW LOOK THROUGH SPIRITUAL PARADIGM

Self Confidence through Hypnosis
Stress Management
Art of Parenting
People Management – an enlightened approach
Creating a Happy Marriage
Hypnosis and Relationship
Living in Freedom – an Enquiry
LIFE series

VIDEO (in VCD form)

Suffering to Surrender
Jokes to Joy – Navarasa
Discouragement to Encouragement
Worry to Wisdom
Stress Management through Spirituality
Seeds of Wisdom
Looking Life Differntly
A Balanced Man
Vedanta – the dynamics of living
Inner Awakening
Harmony in Chaos
Bhagavad Gita – Chapter II (Vol. 1 to 26)

Swamiji's workshop empowers one to be Effective, Creative & Celebrative in all walks of life.

'LIFE' – a two-days workshop on how to use the mind for Success and Satisfaction

---

Objective of the Seminar:

Outer Winner

- The art of powerful goal setting.
- Decision-making, Team building.
- Divine principles of worldly achievement.
- Interpersonal skills & Effective communication
- How to deal with difficult people.
- Possibility thinker.

Inner Winner

- The art of being blissful, restful and loving.
- The art of healing psychological wounds.
- Mind management
- Worry management.
- Fear management.
- Meditation to bring about healthy inner healing and enlightenment.

What others say about the programme:

"Here's one Guru who's in tune with modern times."
— India Today.

"The unusual Swami from Bangalore is the latest Guru on the Indian Management scene."
— Business India.

"He has come to be hailed as the 'Corporate Guru'. The Management Swami has attempted to infuse the Corporate World with the much needed dose of ethics and spirituality."
— The Hindu.

True Freedom Lies
In the Art of Looking at Life Afresh

Glide through work pressures without the 'Sting of Stress'.

Say Yes to Growth, Achievement, Progress
Say No to Stress, Fatigue, Pressure.

Oh, Mind Relax Please!
a one-day workshop

---

on transformation from ordinary to extra-ordinary, dealing with fear & conflicts and converting them as challenges

The programme offers:

- ◆ Impactful models to imbibe powerful insights, to bring forth creativity and spontaneity and discover life nourishing patterns rather than life defeating ones.

- ◆ Practical workouts using sciences of Pranayamas and Mudras as an antidote to the Yuppie Flu.

- ◆ Techniques to debug and update your inner softwares and to gracefully align to change.

- ◆ Processes to synergize a healthy mind with a healthy body.

For more details on Swamiji's in-house & public workshops, contact:

PRASANNA TRUST

51, Ground Floor, 16th Cross,
Between 6th & 8th Main
Malleswaram, Bangalore 560 055, India
Tel: +91 80 2344 4112, 4153 5832-35, Fax: +91 80 2344 4112
E-mail – prasannatrust@vsnl.com
prmadhav@vsnl.com
Visit us at www.swamisukhabodhananda.org

NIRGUNA MANDIR

#1, Nirguna Mandir Layout,
Near I Block Park, Koramangala,
Bangalore – 560 047, INDIA
Phone: (080) 2552 6102

At USA

E-mail: toshakila@hotmail.com

At UK

E-mail: Nisha1507@aol.com

----- ✄ --------------- ✄ ------

Please send me information on

☐ **Seminar on LIFE program**

☐ **Seminar on Oh, Mind Relax Please!**

☐ **Seminar on Corporate Harmony & Creativity at work**

☐ **Books, Audio Cassettes, CD's, VCD's**

Name .... Title ....

Company ....

Address ....

....

City .... State .... Pin ....

Telephone (Off) .... (Res) ....

Fax .... Email ....